COMEBACK

COMEBACK

Jean-Claude Killy
with Al Greenberg

Macmillan Publishing Co., Inc.
NEW YORK

Collier Macmillan Publishers
LONDON

Macmillan Publishing Co., Inc.
866 Third Avenue, New York, N.Y. 10022
Collier-Macmillan Canada Ltd.

First Printing 1974

Printed in the United States of America

Library of Congress Cataloging in Publication Data

Killy, Jean-Claude.
  Comeback.

    1. Killy, Jean-Claude.   2. Ski racing.   I. Greenberg, Al.   II. Title.
  GV854.2.K5A32   796.9'3'0924 [B]   73-18515
  ISBN 0-02-563040-7

For
Danièle

CONTENTS

Introduction   ix

1 Countdown and Flashback   1

2 Contracts and Aftermaths   18

3 Relationships and Existence   42

4 Handicap Racing   63

5 Back on the Circuit   76

6 Lost: The Winning Touch   98

7 Getting It Back   108

8 Michigan Drama   122

9 The Superstars   132

10 Celebrity Race   143

11 Disaster and Victory   156

12 Pull It Off   174

INTRODUCTION

THERE IS A TALE—oft-told at après-ski gatherings—about a fine skier named Jones who, having lived a fruitful life, found himself at the pearly gates. He had no doubt about where he was as soon as he heard St. Peter's cordial greeting: "Did you bring your skis?"

And a skier's heaven it was. Sunshine, azure-blue sky, crystal-clear air, beautiful white snow. Jones looked about him ecstatically.

"How do you like that for a mogul slope?" St. Peter asked, pointing to a long hill covered with a rash of evenly rounded bumps. Among the throngs of delighted skiers boogeying down in the latest hot-dog style, Jones could make out the skiing greats of yesteryear—Snowshoe Thompson, Matthias Zdarsky, Fred Iselin, Sigi Buchmayr. What a sight! Best of all, there was a high-speed gondola lift—with no waiting line!

Looking for a possible hitch, Jones asked, "How about if a guy likes powder?"

"No problem," St. Peter reassured him. "Alta or Snowbird can't hold a candle to what we've got here." And with that, the newcomer was ushered over to another lift and shot almost instantaneously to the top of a mountain of untracked snow —which was curious because Jones thought he had just seen some powder hounds blasting down. "You first," St. Peter offered. So Jones did it, with St. Peter following, intertwining his tracks for perfect figure-eights all the way back to the lift.

"Can we ski that again?" Jones wanted to know.

"As often as you'd like," said St. Peter.

Back up they went—and miracle of miracles, the snow was untracked again. Heaven? You'd better believe it.

Still looking for a flaw, Jones asked, "How about if I want to run slalom gates?"

"This you've got to see," St. Peter told him, and led him off to still another slope. And there *was* a sight. Hannes Schneider, Bud Werner, Charles and Michel Bozon, and other top racers were running these courses, knocking down slalom poles right and left—only to have them spring back up automatically. Fantastic!

Suddenly, Jones detected one disturbing note. "Isn't there some mistake?" he asked in some anguish. "He was so young, too. I just didn't know Jean-Claude Killy had died."

"No, we don't make mistakes," St. Peter answered a little huffily as he consulted his list. "Killy—let's see. No, he's still very much alive. Lives in Geneva."

"Impossible," said Jones. "I'd know that style anywhere. That relaxed stance, arms out for balance. Besides, you can tell—he's a second faster than anyone on the hill."

"Show me who you mean," St. Peter asked curiously.

"There, that guy at the bottom of the hill. That's got to be Jean-Claude Killy—the one signing autographs."

"Oh, *Him,*" St. Peter laughed. "No, that's not Jean-Claude Killy. That's God. He only *thinks* He's Jean-Claude Killy."

This story came to mind as my secretary, Norma Higinbotham (now *Skiing Magazine*'s Travel Editor) helped me transcribe the tapes I had made with Jean-Claude for this book. "Don't you find it hard," she wanted to know, "to write Jean-Claude's story in the first person?"

"Why not at all," I exclaimed in surprise. "After all, when I ski, I always *think* I'm Jean-Claude Killy."

In effect, ever since 1968, all of us recreational types have skied with a mental image of ourselves as Jean-Claude Killy. For Jean-Claude made it look so easy. Not just winning, which he did with a consistency hitherto unknown in the sport, but in the way he handled himself on the slopes. There were no exaggerated mannerisms in the Killy style. Before him, Stein Eriksen's glued-together legs made for the kind of picture-book prettiness no ordinary skier could hope to emulate. "Nobody skis like Stein," the analysts said in admiration; and it was true. But watching Killy, everyone believed he could do the same thing. It was so natural, it was deceptive. For, in fact, nobody *could* ski like Killy—or, at least, nobody could ski that fast. And then the man became a legend. He had won everything, so there was no point in doing it again and again. He went on to other things—making a lot of money. For over four years, he abandoned the race course. Then, in the summer of 1972, the rumor was out: Killy was going to race again. It was hard to believe. Oh, one could easily see why he might want to. After all, Killy made his living from promoting his name, and an active sports figure was certainly more promotable than an ex-sports figure.

But people who know ski racing didn't take it seriously. Killy race again? Maybe after one year, two years off the slopes, a skier could hone down his reflexes, but it would be a hard struggle. Ski races are won and lost by hundredths of a second. To race, you need strength, agility, and machine-like muscular responses developed only after a lifetime of practice. To be away from competition for over four years, as Killy had, would make it virtually impossible to regain a winning form. And for Killy to come back and lose was unthinkable. He would never take that kind of risk.

At least, that's what the smart money said. This is Jean-Claude's story of how wrong they were.

Al Greenberg
Larchmont, N.Y.
October 1973

COMEBACK

1
COUNTDOWN AND FLASHBACK

I AM alone again in the starting gate.

Thousands of times I have stood in this spot, poised, muscles tensed, ready for the start of a ski race. Every time, I have shut out the world and lost myself in total concentration on the course, on the mountain—determined, even certain, that victory would be mine.

But this is different. I'm at Mt. Snow, Vermont, in a race which, at the moment, seems to be the most important of my career.

Were I to utter this thought aloud into the course announcer's microphone, I'm sure it would cause disbelief, perhaps even hilarity, among the fans who know me. How could a race at Mt. Snow, Vermont, be that important to Jean-Claude Killy, a racer who has won everything? On the face of it, the idea does seem absurd: what is Mt. Snow to racing history? This course I'm about to ski is so flat that it's like skiing from the base lodge down to the parking lot. It's not like skiing the Hahnenkamm at Kitzbühel.

The Hahnenkamm. Winning the Hahnenkamm is to a ski racer like winning the Indianapolis 500 is to a racing car driver or like winning at Wimbledon is to a tennis pro. For a young skier, just to be there is the fulfillment of a dream. How I wanted to win that race back in 1965! I was still relatively unknown then. Though I had won some fairly important races,

*such as the giant slalom at the Critérium de la Première Neige
at Val d'Isère in 1961 and the Kandahar giant slalom at Garm-
isch-Partenkirchen in 1964, when I got to Kitzbühel in 1965
I still had not taken a first on any of the major international
courses.*

*I skied well in the first run (in standard slalom racing, every-
one goes through two courses; the skier with the lowest combined time for the two runs wins), but I was still about a half
second behind the leader—Karl Schranz of Austria. I remember,
the tip of my ski hit one of the slalom poles and I just avoided
a disqualification by a fraction of an inch. I interpreted the fact
that I was still in the race as a sign that I was going to have a
good day. In the second run, I shot out of the starting gate
positive I was going to win. I was told that when Schranz saw
me taking the first few gates his face turned white. It must really
have shaken him up because I not only overcame his lead, I
won by almost two seconds. I had run a perfect race. The surge
of emotion that burst through me, the pounding in my head, the
delirium—there is just no way I can describe the intensity of the
joy that overwhelmed me with that victory. For I had not just
proved that I could win, but that I could take the Hahnenkamm,
the most prestigious race of them all.*

Yes, I am all alone in this starting gate, even though there is
another racer alongside of me. His name is Malcolm Milne,
an Australian who had been a good downhiller on the amateur
circuit. I had stayed at his house in Australia after his older
brother, Ross, was killed in a downhill race. Malcolm was sixteen and wanted to go to Europe to race, to take up where his
brother had left off. His parents wouldn't hear of it but they
finally agreed when I promised to look after him. Technically
he is not a good slalom skier, but this course is ideal for him—
not the kind he faced as an amateur. For this is a professional
race, a totally different format from what both of us had known.

Almost five years after winning three gold medals as an amateur in the Olympic Games at Grenoble, I am again racing. But
I have yet to have my first winning day as a pro, and it is
important to me that I succeed. I am concentrating on the course,

not even aware that the starting gate here looks more like a horse-racing stall than the traditional wand I am used to, the wand that starts the timing device going the moment your legs push it aside. On the pro circuit, you don't race against the clock, you race against the skier on the next course—*dual slalom* they call it. The heavy metal starting gates open simultaneously so the two racers start off together. If there's an advantage, it's to the man with the faster reflexes.

But I am not worrying about the gate, and I have forgotten that Malcolm is alongside me. The solitude I feel as I study this flat course is just as though I were all alone at the start of one of the classic downhills—long, steep, terrifying. I am concentrating just as I would for skiing the Hahnenkamm downhill, or the Piste Verte at Chamonix or the Piste Emile Allais at Megève. I am paying no attention to anyone around the starting gate, and I'm not thinking the gates are set differently or that the surroundings are a far cry from, let us say, Wengen, Switzerland.

"Wait till Wengen." That's what the Austrians said after I won the FIS (Fédération Internationale de Ski) championship downhill at Portillo, Chile, in 1966. That was my first downhill victory in international competition, and a lot of people thought it was a fluke. So in 1967 I was anxious to get to Wengen to ski the Lauberhorn downhill. If you saw Robert Redford in Downhill Racer, *which was shot at Wengen, you may remember what the area looks like. You are at the foot of the Eiger, which is perhaps the most frightening and yet the most beautiful mountain I know. You can see the mountain train going up the Jungfrau, unloading thousands of skiers above timberline. At the top of that run, you feel like a very small human being lost in a very big world of craggy, snow-covered peaks. When the weather is right, there isn't another race course in the world with such a panorama for a backdrop. But what makes the Lauberhorn tough is that it is so long and the weather is frequently so bad that you must have the right wax and stamina as well as the technique. It has been run since 1930, with such names as Toni Sailer, Christian Pravda, Karl Schranz, and*

Henri Duvillard among the winners. And in 1967, Jean-Claude Killy—a full second ahead of Egon Zimmermann. I had proved my Portillo win was no fluke, and though I didn't get the same kind of emotional charge I got from my first big win at Kitz-bühel or from my first downhill win at Portillo, in my memory the grandeur of the Wengen landscape is inseparable from my pride at winning the Lauberhorn.

Though I'm familiar with many ski areas in the United States, this was the first time I had visited Mt. Snow. I love to go to a new place, even if it's only twenty kilometers from my house. The chance to visit so many new places was part of the attraction for me in attempting a comeback. And Mt. Snow was certainly very different from any ski area I had ever seen. I was staying at the Snow Lake Lodge, an unusual hotel in many ways. It has Japanese pools and tropical plants in the lobby, with girls in bikinis around the pools. A small air car—a tiny *téléphérique,* really—that leaves from the lobby takes skiers over a lake to the slopes. I was told that the lake used to have a fountain in it that was modeled after the fountain in Lake Geneva. It wasn't operating when the racers arrived, which was too bad; I would have felt right at home since I can see the fountain in Lac Leman (as we French call it) from my home in Geneva.

Mt. Snow gets very crowded, everyone says, and I can see why. The food was as good as any I've ever eaten at an American ski area, and there are some very nice slopes, too. The first day we arrived, I tried out some new skis on what they call the North Face, which has some fairly steep runs. It is too far from the lodge for racing, and not the kind of terrain that would be suitable for a professional course, but it was very enjoyable. In the afternoon, as the sun drops behind the hilltop, the backlighting of skiers throwing up little sprays of powder is picture-postcard pretty. Mt. Snow also has a heated outdoor swimming pool and an artificially cooled indoor ice-skating rink. It has lots of chair lifts which criss-cross one another, something like the lift system at Tignes, the area adjoining my native Val d'Isère. Some American skiers call Mt. Snow skiing's Coney Island; the ambiance is certainly unique.

But today the crowd at this race is far smaller than anticipated—perhaps 2,000 people. It is cold, bitter, biting cold, and as I stand in the starting gate, my friend Michel Arpin finishes rubbing my arms and legs to warm my muscles. Michel has been my constant companion and trainer since early in my amateur days when he left the French team to go to work for Dynamic Skis. One of those rare individuals who combines dedication to the point of perfectionism with a high level of theoretical and technical proficiency, Michel was my secret weapon when I was dominating the amateur ski circuit, and though I have shut even him out of my awareness as I stand in the gate, I depend on him fully. He wears the same boot size as I do and he has analyzed my skiing style so well, he can test and prepare my equipment so that I can get the last shred of performance out of each piece of gear I use. Without him, I probably never could have won two World Cups or three gold medals at Grenoble.

At Grenoble, I was the local favorite. That was to be expected, with the Winter Olympics being held on French soil. My uncle, who owns a construction company in Alsace, had given all his workers two days off so they could attend, and they were all there holding big signs from their firm, Killy Frères. But it wasn't just these personal touches: General de Gaulle was there; the whole French nation, in fact, was expecting me to win everything because I had had such a fantastic season in 1966–67, winning all the downhills on the circuit. For close observers of the racing scene, though, the real favorite in the downhill at Grenoble was the Austrian, Gerhard Nenning. He was hot, and I hadn't won a single downhill in 1968 prior to Grenoble. Then, in the nonstop practice run, Michel Arpin's stopwatch gave me some confidence: I had the fastest time. Besides, I heard that Nenning had broken his skis and was looking for another pair. That could be a serious handicap for him, and naturally, when I heard about it, I felt my chances had improved. But just when I was feeling most optimistic, disaster struck. A half hour before the race, I skied over a patch of ice and ruined my wax. I had scratched my ski bottoms so that the care-

fully selected protective wax coating was practically gone. In desperation, I looked everywhere for Michel, but I couldn't find him. Finally, when he appeared, it was too late to rewax. "Don't worry," he said. "I've been down the course. You'll win anyway. Just get a good start." Later, he told me he didn't believe there was any way I could make up for the bad condition of my ski bottoms. "But up there at the top, it wasn't the moment to tell you," he explained. Nevertheless, I believed him, though I knew I had to go all out, that it was impossible to win unless I took every chance in the book. With the wax problem I had and the handicap of a late starting number—which might have been an advantage in good weather but was a penalty in the fog and snow we had at Grenoble—the only way I could win was to ski without a mistake. I had a fantastic run all right and did manage to win—though only by .08 of a second. When I realized I had done it, I knew these were going to be my Olympic Games.

I've been in plenty of cold weather—you can't be a skier and encounter nothing but sunshine and mild temperatures. But I've never passed a colder night than the one preceding this day of the giant slalom race. I was rooming with Alain Penz, a former member of the French team. As an amateur, Alain had twice been number one in the World Cup slalom standings. I had a bottle of champagne in the room; I intended to open it to celebrate my first victory—tonight, I hoped. Suddenly, we were awakened by a loud noise. Alain jumped out of bed looking for I don't know what—an intruder, a practical joker. "That sounded like a gun," I said as I turned on the light to look at my watch. My hand was shaking so from the cold, I could scarcely make out the time. It was 2 A.M.

"There's your gun," Alain said, pointing to the champagne bottle. I couldn't believe it. The temperature in the room had dropped so low, the champagne had frozen and the bottle had exploded! That was the noise we had heard.

"Can't you turn up the heater?" I asked Alain.

"You turn it up. I'm getting out of here. I'm going to sleep in Michel's room," he said, hurrying off as though he were afraid I would race him to Michel's room where we knew there was an extra bed.

I didn't feel like wandering around the hotel in my pajamas looking for another place to sleep, so after fooling with the radiator to no avail—it just wasn't working—I took all of Alain's blankets, sheets, and pillows and piled them on my bed. I still wasn't warm enough, so I got up once again and put on my winter underwear. I was still cold—it must have been twenty below in the room—so I got up again and put on my warmup pants, socks, parka, gloves, and hat—and even then I couldn't sleep. When it was time to get up, I was all dressed to go skiing.

And I had to be ready at Mt. Snow. There had been two pro races earlier this season—the first at Aspen, the second at Vail, Colorado. *Sports Illustrated* had run a very encouraging article about my return to competition, but I had not done well at Aspen, and though I had done a little better at Vail, the press I had received was bad: "Killy Beaten by Aging Ski Instructors" and things like that. First of all, it wasn't true. The winners of the first races, Harald Stuefer, Hugo Nindl, and Spider Sabich were all top pros, full-time racers, not part-time instructors. And among the leaders were young racers fresh out of the amateurs —Alain Penz, Tyler Palmer, Dan Mooney, Hank Kashiwa, Pierre Pouteil-Noble, Malcolm Milne, Perry Thompson, and lots more. Actually, in the overall standings, I wasn't doing so badly coming into Mr. Snow—I was third behind Harald Stuefer and Alain Penz, and actually tied for second in earnings.

If any other ski racer had come out of retirement and had performed this well after being away from competition for four years, people would have said, "Wait till he gets back on his skis. He'll clean up." But that wasn't the way the commentators reacted to my first race at Aspen, which, I suppose, is understandable, given my reputation. What is less understandable is that some of the other competitors rushed into print with similarly disparaging observations. The American Tyler Palmer, for example, talked about my having too much upper body motion, as though that were part of my style of skiing. Michel and I were well aware that I had too much upper body motion. I knew I was making a lot of mistakes. I hadn't even selected the skis and boots I was going to be using. And I certainly wasn't familiar with the pro format. It should have been obvious to everyone that I couldn't be off skis for such a long time and then return to competition skiing as well as I used to. So I was angry at some of the things that were being said about me and it caused me to try harder at Vail. I still wasn't skiing well, but I did better: a second and a fourth.

But a second for me is nothing. I have to be first. It is not just a matter of pride, or even money. I'm never apologetic about the money. I'm a professional, and skiing is my business. But to me, ski racing is also an art form. When I'm racing, I'm not there to hear the crowd yelling or to achieve glory or to earn money. I'm there to ski a perfect race. The artist who paints a picture likes to get money for it, likes to win the approval of the critics and the adulation of the public. But that's not why he creates his work of art. He doesn't need spectators to watch him paint. His primary pleasure is derived from the pure act of creation. So, too, the pleasure I receive from ski racing is pure; instead of canvas, palette, paint, and painter, the elements are snow, speed, skis, and skier. Not every first-place finish is a work of art in ski racing; but *only* a first can be.

I was not only dissatisfied with my first professional results, I had doubts about the wisdom of what I was doing. A return to competition made sense only if I again dominated the sport. When I retired, there was no question I was the best. Having made a name, I had done well merchandising it. Now, if I were to be less than best, my business interests would suffer. And I was no longer sure I could ski the perfect race; no longer sure, even, that I could ski faster than the others.

It was Michel Arpin who, the preceding summer, had persuaded me that I should attempt a comeback; Michel and my fiancée, Danièle Gaubert. Danièle sensed that my happiest moments were associated with my ski racing life. She became interested in my returning to this life when we read that Spider Sabich had won over $50,000 in prize money on the Grand Prix circuit and that Benson & Hedges, the sponsors, planned to put up more money in the 1972–73 season. She thought it would make sense for me from a business point of view—that my name would become more marketable—and that, therefore, it would be worth my while to spend the time training and racing. But first of all, for her, it was a question of what she thought would make me happiest. She just assumed I could win—easily, in fact.

For Michel, it was different. When I turned professional and signed a contract with Head Ski Co., Michel came along as technical consultant. Later, he went on the amateur race circuit for Head, preparing skis for American racers. Well, I think he hated it. It seems to me that he hates to work with losers. These skiers weren't trying one hundred percent, and he wanted to work again with someone who would try. He knew that if I decided to race again, I would try, and he thought I could win. He was convinced that ski racing technique hadn't progressed much since I had been on the circuit. He would get into a lot of fights about that. He would say, well, Killy was better than that. Whether it was Penz or Russel or Augert, he would say these guys still aren't skiing as well as Killy did three years ago. And guys like René Sulpice or Jean Beranger, coaches of the French team, would laugh at him, and this disturbed him. The trainers and the journalists all seemed to agree that ski racing had advanced way beyond where it had been in my day.

Anyway, he came to my house in Geneva to tell me about these things, figuring I would be persuaded that there might be good money in it and that I would be tempted to prove not only that the Killy of 1968 was better than the skiers of today, but that an older, less-conditioned Killy was still better than the rest. Frankly, I thought he was crazy. I had considered ski racing to be a closed page in my life. I loved it, but I wasn't sure I wanted to devote my life to it again, not at all sure that I wanted to lift weights all day and ride my bike on top of mountains to get back into shape. But Michel kept working on me, and I got caught up with the idea.

At first, we thought we could have open skiing—you know, pros and amateurs competing together as in tennis or golf. That would have pitted me against the top amateurs on the World Cup circuit as well as professionals who were big drawing cards.

I had lunch with Marc Hodler, the president of the FIS, and he was all for it, and it looked very good. When I started training that summer, it seemed that we would get approval for open skiing. But the French and Austrian ski federations shot us down. Well, I didn't want all that training to go to waste. I had been bitten by the comeback bug, so now it was a matter of looking around to see where I could compete. Frankly, I didn't consider the Beattie tour at first. I had great respect for Bob Beattie, whom I knew from his days as head coach for the U.S. ski team. But his International Ski Racers Association (ISRA) circuit sounded like a circus to me—and a two-bit circus at that. My managers tried to put a Killy–Schranz tour together, but neither Karl Schränz nor I was very interested in that kind of format. I wanted to race against everybody, not just one man. Then I heard that a lot of young racers were joining Beattie's organization, which made it a completely different ball game.

This came to my attention in a funny way. Gérard Rubaud of Rossignol Skis came to visit me in Geneva to ask me to be manager–coach of the Rossignol team. The racers on the team were Alain Penz, Otto Tschudi, Malcolm Milne, and Pierre Pouteil-Noble. As I've mentioned, Penz, twenty-five, had twice tied for the World Cup slalom title and was a member of the French A team. Tschudi, twenty-three, was a Norwegian who had won five NCAA titles at Denver University. Milne, twenty-four, was the Australian who was a top-ranked downhiller. And Pouteil-Noble, twenty-two, was a member of the French B team.

I was impressed. First, I was impressed that Rossignol would consider the Beattie tour important enough to field a factory team. More important, I figured that if Beattie's tour could attract not only established racers like Penz and Milne, but also young racers with no reputation—racers like Tschudi and Pouteil-Noble—but who had a potential to win and a desire to make a name for themselves in racing, then that tour would be a success. So I told Rubaud how glad I was that Beattie's circuit was not just a bunch of former champions. However, I also told him that I wasn't much of a manager and didn't feel I was ready to coach. Instead, I told him I was going to race myself.

His response floored me. He simply said, "Rossignol isn't

interested in you as a racer, Jean-Claude. You're too old and you haven't been on your skis. Technique today isn't what it used to be when you were racing. Everyone skis faster. You'd have no chance at all. We don't think you can win." That shook me up all right and caused a lot of second thoughts during the rest of the summer and fall. I must add, though, that Rubaud came to me after my race at Aspen, where I thought I was skiing terribly, and apologized. "I made the biggest mistake of my life," he said. "But at least I'm smart enough to admit it. If you ski like this after such a short time back on snow, I can see you're going to have a successful comeback."

Then it was my turn to apologize: "I thought you were just a racer-chaser, but I see now you are much more than that."

To tell the truth, I had known Rubaud for a good number of years and only now did I discover how much I had misjudged him. I first met him in 1955 at a training camp in Valloire. He was a good skier and mountain climber, though in competition he had never gone any further than the regional championships. When he quit racing, he went to work for Rossignol and also went back to school to take some business courses. If he wasn't the first racer-chaser—that is, if he didn't actually invent the job—he certainly completely changed the nature of it.

Loosely speaking, a racer-chaser is any factory representative who follows the competitors on the race circuit to service skiers who use his company's equipment. When Rubaud first started doing this, Michel and I had no use for him. We felt he wasn't half the technician Michel was, and we thought he was just an opportunist exploiting his position with a big company. What we didn't realize was that Gérard didn't *have* to be a good technician. His strength lay in organization. He could always find competent guys to wax skis or file edges.

Rubaud saw racer-chasing as a combination of selling, promotion, and service. He would convince the top skiers to use Rossignol, and then he would see to it that they stayed happy. He had a big budget and knew how to use it creatively—not just in finding competent shopmen to do the waxing, edge sharpening, flat filing, or repair work. He would also do things like taking Mike Lafferty, the American downhiller, and arranging for him to study French so he could train with the French Team. At one point, when the French Team was badly disorganized, Gérard took over the organizational details for the whole team —not just for those on Rossignol. He made the hotel reservations for everyone, handled the transportation, saw that everyone's skis were properly prepared; in effect, he was the coach. Because he was so good at this kind of thing, he became a very powerful force on the racing scene and had much to do with the success of Rossignol.

But I had had no contact with him between 1968 and the summer of 1972. Initially, one of the reasons I wasn't very interested in using Rossignol skis was that I thought Michel would never be able to work with Gérard. Then, at Tignes, before the first race, we ran into the Rossignol Team members —saw that there indeed was such a team, saw how they trained, and how all had contracts arranged by Rubaud. Where before I thought Rubaud was just some kind of clown, I now realized he was a sound businessman who knew what he was doing. I was impressed, too, with his prescience because, I must say, he was one of the few who saw me ski at Aspen who understood that my performance wasn't all that bad considering how little I had skied beforehand.

Michel, of course, never lost faith in me. But at Aspen, even he began to have doubts. Not over whether I could do it. He just thought maybe it would take longer for me to get back into shape, to regain my old form, and particularly my old aggressiveness, than he at first imagined. The turning point for *him* was Vail. There, though I was disappointed with my second place finish, Michel was really pleased. He decided then and there that I was going to win the Grand Prix. He figured it might take me till the middle of February before I put it all together and won a whole day's races, but after Vail, he was supremely confident. If I could do that well with only ten days of skiing —that's all the on-snow training I had had before Aspen—he was certain that more training would put me on top. And there was going to be time for that. There was to be a month's layoff between the Vail race and Mt. Snow, a month that we would use to get in shape, to get the right equipment, to regain balance and reflexes lost after four years of a different life.

But I wasn't so sure. Only a victory could prove to me that I still had what it takes. I had worked hard to get it all back, but the big question in my mind was whether I could sustain my form for nine runs in a row. That was what was required under the pro format. Forty racers start out in time trials for what is known as the qualifying round. Only sixteen qualify. Today, cold as I had been in my freezing room, I started out hot. I had the fastest qualifying run—almost a full second ahead of anyone else. In amateur racing, a qualification round is run only for the World Championships and the Olympics. It is designed to give lower-seeded racers—particularly those from small countries—who can't get to enough big races to improve their seeding a chance to compete on more equal terms with the top-seeded racers. If the top racers take it too lightly, it could result in their disqualification, but otherwise, the effect of the qualification round in the amateurs is mostly psychological. For example, Carlo Senoner, the Italian racer who won the FIS slalom championship at Portillo, Chile, in 1966, had never won a major slalom before. But he got such a boost from his good showing in the qualification round that he went on to win.

In professional racing, this same psychological effect is possible—it certainly gave me a boost—but the qualification round is much more important. First, if you're not among the first sixteen you're automatically out of the race. Second, the racer you face in the opening round and in each succeeding round is determined by your showing in the qualifying run. The two best times are paired up with the two worst times, and so forth. The qualifying round is run against the clock. Thereafter, you face one opponent, and it's man to man, side by side on two courses as nearly identical as the course setters can make them. After the first run, to make sure it's equal, you switch courses. The racer with the best combined times on the two runs wins and goes on to face a winner of one of the other head-to-head contests, the order depending on your position on the ladder—that is to say, on your time in the qualifying round.

So, here at Mt. Snow, my first opponent after the qualifying round was a relatively weak skier, a young Canadian named Bert Irwin. The only difficulty I had was keeping warm between runs. When Michel wasn't rubbing my legs or arms, I'd be jumping up and down or waving my arms—but I couldn't get warm; it was the preceding night all over again. I really felt sorry for the people standing around to watch.

In the quarterfinals, I was not so lucky. My opponent was Spider Sabich, who had beaten Otto Tschudi in the opening round. Spider was a Californian who had been a member of the U.S. team but who had been plagued with accidents as an amateur. He occasionally showed flashes of talent on the international circuit, but he was too erratic to make it to the top. In the slalom at the Grenoble Olympics, he was the best American, placing fifth. Two years later, he joined the Beattie circuit where he suddenly came into his own. Not only was he the big money winner two years in a row, he built up a following and became the big name in the sport. A tall, good-looking, well-built man with wavy blond hair, he had the kind of flamboyant personality journalists like to write about. In the summer, he likes to ride a motorcycle and flies his own twin-engine Piper Aztec. He has an easy-going manner with the public and handles himself well with the press. A lot of journalists were already talking about the current pro season as a Killy-Sabich duel. Meeting him face-to-face here at Mt. Snow was a challenge for me, and the TV men couldn't have been happier.

Oh, yes, this race was being televised. ABC's Wide World of Sports was there in force—this was the first race of the season to get this attention. My old friend Jim McKay, anchorman for this sports series, was there, and I was very pleased to see him again. I had known him at Portillo and Grenoble. If I'm not mistaken, he was the first man to interview me on American television. Here at Mt. Snow, the night before this race, Jim again had me before the camera, sort of a fireside chat about my plans and why I had started racing again and how I expected to do. I told him I was confident, that I had worked very hard, and that I would try to do well, which, of course, was all I could say. But I had the impression that this telecast was to be more a Killy show than a pro-racing show, with a scene from my movie *Snow Job,* and this interview, which was fairly long. So with all this extra attention, I was particularly anxious to perform well.

I imagine Spider was just as anxious. Everyone realizes the importance of television to the success of professional sports. In fact, the official starting time of the race was changed from 1:30 P.M. to 1 P.M. because the cameramen were afraid the light would be bad by the time the finals rolled around. But even television isn't all-powerful. It was so cold that the timing devices had frozen, and it wasn't until 1:40 that they had them thawed out enough to start the race.

This flat course was not to Spider's liking. The spectator is apt to think that a flat course is easier to ski than a steep course. But no world-class competitor worries about handling the steep. The difficulty on a flat course is that if you make a mistake and lose your speed, there's no way to recover. That's what happened to Spider. Coming off a bump, he lost his line, and I just sped past him to win.

In the semifinals, I faced Perry Thompson, one of several young Americans I had never heard of before joining the pro tour. Perry had beaten Tyler Palmer in the opening round and Mike Schwaiger, an Austrian pro, in the quarterfinals, so even though I knew very little about him, it was evident he was skiing well that day. Besides, I was beginning to get tired. Unlike most of the racers, I had had no vacation between Christmas and New Years. I had trained hard all month, gone back to Geneva on December 31, had some champagne to celebrate the arrival of the new year, then flown out the next day and had to adjust to the six-hour time difference. All during our stay at Mt. Snow, I had been interviewed constantly, so again, I had had little time to rest. And then this sleepless night in the cold. Could I hold out?

I couldn't let myself think otherwise. I forced myself to concentrate on the course, and again I won. Meantime, Malcolm Milne was facing Hank Kashiwa. Kashiwa, a former U.S. team member, had joined the pro tour late the previous season. His technique was sound, and he promised to be a threat. Kashiwa, by the way, was one competitor who didn't jump to conclusions after my Aspen performance. He told Michel Arpin at the time that he knew I was going to be the man to beat.

The others in the quarterfinals were new to the circuit this year. I remembered that it was the presence of these new skiers that had persuaded me to join the Beattie tour, and now it looked as though the newcomers were taking over. After the first race at Aspen, the leader in the overall standings was Alain Penz. Others new to the pros were also right up in the first ten —youngsters like Pouteil-Noble and Ken Corrock. Even though I was an old-timer at racing, I felt I was a rookie here, and I was sure we rookies were going to take over the pro circuit this season. That would be all for Sabich, Stuefer, and Nindl.

Milne beat Kashiwa in his end of the semifinals, and now I am facing him and I'm no longer tired, no longer cold. The starter says, "Skiers ready?" and I *am* ready. I no longer have any doubts. I am the confident Killy: the triple gold medal winner of Grenoble, the two-time World Cup winner, the conqueror of the Hahnenkamm and the Lauberhorn, the owner of the Arlberg-Kandahar diamond, the U.S. and French champion. My positive attitude extends to my skiing, and I win the first run easily. For the second run, my head is already pounding in anticipation. Again, I shoot out of the starting gate, skating to pick up speed. The snow under my skis is squeaky from the cold. I take the jump with my shoulders square to the skis— reversing them would mean losing time on the next turn. In and out of the gates I go, carving my turns, straightening out the course, carrying my speed through the flat. Near the finish, I know I'm ahead and I glance back over my shoulder to see the kind of margin I have. It's all over! I straighten up and go through the finish raising my poles in triumph.

Bob Beattie interviews me on television, and I can't express what I feel. No one would believe it anyway. It's the biggest moment in my life. I felt like this at Kitzbühel in my first Hahnenkamm victory, and at Portillo when I won my first big downhill. An inside explosion. A dream that I worked hard for has come true, and everything has turned red. Everything around me is going in slow motion. I have proved my point, and my blood is literally exploding in my head.

They are pulling me to the winner's stand and the people are swarming around me. I search out Michel Arpin, for this is his victory, too. He has devoted so much of himself—all his time since September—and I have proved that he was right, that I could do this.

I don't believe it's possible to get this feeling in any other walk of life. A businessman signing an important contract may be elated, but he can't have the emotional exhilaration I'm talking about because the same kind of physical commitment hasn't preceded it. Some people report they get this kind of high from drugs. I've had no experience with drugs, and although I've heard there are some ski racers who use drugs, as far as I've been able to observe it doesn't help them ski any better. I know it doesn't help them beat me. In any event, my high comes from victory. Sports are my drugs. And these specially significant victories—at Kitzbühel, at Portillo, and now here at Mt. Snow—are my mainliners. I am sorry for those who cannot experience the same thing.

This glow, this intense orgy of happiness, lasts only a few minutes. You are still happy as you come back into the real world, but you temper that happiness with the realization that there are other goals waiting to be achieved. I had won my first professional race. But I hadn't undertaken a comeback to prove I could win one race. To tell the truth, I had decided at Aspen that I was on this tour for the whole season, but I hadn't said so to anyone, not even to Michel. He knew it, too, but he didn't say anything to me either. We kept talking about "if" I continued on the tour, "if" I raced at this area or that one, "if" I were in contention for the Grand Prix, and so on. Now that I had won one race, I didn't mind owning up to my plans for the season: I was going to go all the way; I intended to take the Grand Prix.

2
CONTRACTS AND AFTERMATHS

UNTIL the spring of 1968, ski racing had been my entire life. Though I was born in St. Cloud, a suburb of Paris—my family was living nearby at the time, in Courbevoie, where my father was selling bicycles—I grew up in the mountains. My father was originally from the Vosges Mountains in Alsace; my grandfather had been in the construction business there. But my father didn't care for that kind of life, and when I was only three years old, we moved to Val d'Isère, which was then a very small ski resort.

I can't remember when I wasn't a skier. I remember traveling by bus to race at Thollon-les-Memises when I was only seven or eight, and thinking how privileged I was to get to travel. By that time, I had already won my Chamois d'Or—a proficiency medal awarded by the ski school where everyone races against a time set by a ski instructor who has previously been ranked according to his time against other ski instructors (something like the NASTAR races in the United States). On that occasion I beat my instructor by better than a second.

I was only sixteen years old when Honoré Bonnet, coach of the French team, had me training with the A team. In that year, 1960, at La Clusaz, I had swept the French Junior Championships, winning the special slalom, giant slalom, downhill, and combined. The following year, I became an official member of the team. Except for my period in the army—I served in Algeria during the ill-fated war there to preserve French sovereignty in North Africa—the life of the ski racer was all I knew.

It was a fantastic life, but I had nothing else to compare it to. So at the time, I really didn't understand how great it was—the camaraderie, the traveling, the notoriety, and all with really no responsibilities. Some racers complain about the grind, but for me, going from one hotel to the next, from one ski area to another, from one part of the world to distant lands was just wonderful. I didn't need a secretary to make my room reservations. I didn't have to worry about paying the hotel or travel bills. The only activity expected of me was to get on a pair of skis on a mountain and to go as fast as I could from the top to the bottom. In effect, I was not a man, I was a ward of the French Ski Federation. One wouldn't want to live all his days that way, but looking back on it, it was a Garden of Eden. People looked after my diet, my health, my clothes, my training, and my itinerary. If I didn't want to see someone, there was no obligation, no business necessity. I could simply say, "I'm sorry, I have no time to see you. I'm busy skiing." That was all I had to do—to ski, to ski well—and it was really great. I mean the life itself, not whether I won or lost. Winning, of course, was what justified it.

And I won a lot. After sweeping the French Junior Championships in 1960, I won my first international race with a slalom victory at the Grand Prix de Morzine in January 1961. Again I won the French Junior Championship in giant slalom, and the following December, I placed first in the giant slalom at the Critérium de la Première Neige in Val d'Isère, usually the first big international event of every season. In that race, I started thirty-ninth. Starting positions in amateur ski racing are determined by what are known as FIS points. You earn low FIS points by beating other low-seeded skiers. It's a long process that usually requires years of competing in the big races. The best racers are in what is called the first seed—that is, the first fifteen racers. The second seed consists of the next fifteen racers, and so on. Within each seed, you draw lots for starting positions, and then in slalom (and now also in giant slalom) you reverse the order within each seed for a second run.

The reason for all these complicated regulations governing starting order is that as a course is skied on by one skier after another, ruts develop from the skiers turning in the snow at the same places. It is usually a big handicap to start late. Normally, the spectators and journalists start to leave the course after the first seed has run. At that 1961 Critérium, though, my coach, Honoré Bonnet, told the journalists not to leave too early. "Just this once, wait for the third seed," he said. "When number thirty-nine comes through, you're going to see something!" I lived up to his promise. Not only did I win, which in itself is unusual with such a starting number, I was more than a second ahead of my nearest rival. Because they are usually so close, ski races are recorded in hundredths of seconds. Considering my starting position, the margin I had was almost like winning a 100-yard dash by ten yards. Everyone was immediately predicting a very bright future for me.

Soon afterward, though, I suffered a serious setback. The FIS Championships were to be held that winter at Chamonix, and I wanted to improve my FIS points to have a good starting position in every race. I didn't know it, but Bonnet had already decided to qualify me as number one in the giant slalom. Not knowing this, I went all out to get a good result in a downhill that was held in early January at Cortina d'Ampezzo. Again I was in the third seed—I had a forty-three for my starting number—and again I thought I could pull a miracle. I startled everyone by recording the best time at the halfway point, where I was two seconds ahead. But it was a terrible course. Near the end, there were three gates to slow you down. I told myself that if I schussed those last three gates, I would win. The trouble was, right after those gates, there was a big jump and you had to turn left in the air. And I couldn't do it. It was a desperation gamble, and I lost. I fell and broke my right ankle, which put me out of competition for the rest of the year.

Shortly afterward I had to do my army service. I had set my sights on the FIS World Championships at Chamonix where two of my friends from Val d'Isère, Christine and Marielle Goitschel, did so well in the women's races, but my injury kept me out of that. Except for a short period when I served in Algeria my army service didn't interfere much with my skiing. My army assignment was to continue skiing and the following year, I had some good results—I won the combined at the French Championships at Barèges, took first in slalom and combined in the international military championships at Chamonix, and came in second in the Arlberg-Kandahar downhill at Chamonix, the Adelboden giant slalom, the Grand Prix de Megève downhill, and the giant slalom at the Critérium.

In the next year, 1964, I took part in my first Olympics, held at Innsbruck, Austria. Technically, I think I was skiing well enough to have won some medals there, but I didn't have a winning attitude. I was careless in preparing my equipment, I wasn't strong enough physically, and I was too impressed by other racers. Consequently, I lacked the confidence necessary to ski aggressively. My best result at the Innsbruck Games was a fifth in giant slalom. Later that season, I won the French Championships at Méribel, taking firsts in slalom, giant slalom, and combined. I was also first in the Arlberg-Kandahar giant slalom at Garmisch. But I really wasn't in good health, and it wasn't till after an examination by some specialists in sports medicine at the St. Michel Hospital in Paris that I began effective treatment. It turned out that my condition had been diagnosed incorrectly. I had been told I was suffering from jaundice; in fact, my problem was amebic dysentery, which I had caught in Algeria.

One of the things that stands out in my memory of this period was a trip I took to the United States to visit Jimmy Heuga, who had won a bronze medal in slalom at Innsbruck. Jimmy and I had become very good friends, and he had arranged to have me invited to attend an American training camp at Bend, Oregon. The American girls' team was there at the time and I was very impressed with their rigorous program. What impressed me most about the Americans, though, was that they regarded skiing simply as a sport. Most of them were continuing their college careers at the same time that they were on the international circuit. Jimmy was certainly as good as I was then; he had been skiing fantastically that season. And his teammate Bill Kidd, also a college student, had won a silver medal at Innsbruck. I wondered whether the French approach—to pull skiers out of school and have them concentrate on the sport—was the right way. I think the poor results that the American men have had in recent years, as compared to the Europeans, show that my doubts at the time were not well-founded. But in 1964, I had not yet achieved very much, and I was concerned about my future. Having left school as a teenager with a pair of skis as my only baggage, my prospects at that point didn't seem as bright as those of my American counterparts.

The following season, however, my fortunes began to change. For one thing, my health had improved. Most important, though, this was the year Michel Arpin, though still on the French team, became technical advisor for Dynamic. Michel and I first became friends when I joined the team in 1961. He was from Val d'Isère too and used to pick me up in his car. He knew I didn't like to spend time on my equipment, so one day, he came up to me and proposed, "Jean-Claude, since you're skiing on Dynamics, I'll take care of all your equipment needs. All you'll have to do is ski." He would even help me with my Rossignols until he could get Dynamic to make skis as good.

No one I had ever met knew more about equipment than Michel, so naturally I accepted. This meant that on the morning of a race, instead of getting up early and preparing my equipment as everyone else was doing, I could get a couple of extra hours of sleep, confident that no one would have skis prepared any better than mine. Michel wasn't just a ski mechanic. He was still a very good racer, particularly in slalom. In fact, that year, at the Harriman Cup slalom in Sun Valley, he beat me out for first, which I didn't mind at all because Karl Schranz came in third. Later, after an auto accident, Michel had to stop racing, which gave him more time to analyze my skiing, correct errors he saw, time me to find out which skis were fastest, take interval times for me during a race, watch the other racers to see the places on the course where they were having difficulty, and perform a host of other services that were absolutely invaluable to me.

And on top of everything else, I liked him enormously. I liked his frank speech, his sincerity, and the enthusiastic smile that would light up his weatherbeaten face when he was pleased. Not only did we work well together, we enjoyed relaxing together. He was as much fun to be with after skiing as he was helpful while we were skiing.

"Michel, I'll race you back to Val d'Isére, d'accord?"

"No way that Peugeot of yours can keep up with my Matra Jet," he said, and we were off. In those days, that long, winding road from Cannes was empty and there was no speed limit. I had managed to gain the lead. It was raining and the pavement was slick. Suddenly, there was this long curve to the right with trees on the right side and a sharp embankment on the left with nothing to keep you out of the ditch except a single apple tree. I went into a skid, fought it, and finally regained control. I looked in my mirror to see how Michel was doing.

He not only skidded sideways, he did a complete 360. I saw him spinning, and then his car disappeared from my mirror. "He's dead," I thought. I stopped and ran back, and there were apples all over the road. His car had gone into the ditch and smacked into the tree. When I got to him, the car was lying on its roof, wheels spinning in the air, and Michel was unconscious. I dragged him out and took him to the hospital. He was unconscious for two days. It was a year before he regained his equilibrium; for a period, he even lost his memory.

Though the accident ended his ski racing, Michel is still like me: he can't help driving fast. In 1972, he destroyed a Porsche and spent several days in the hospital.

I started the 1964–65 season with second place finishes in downhill and giant slalom at the Critérium. Then I got a second in the Lauberhorn slalom at Wengen and a second in the Arlberg-Kandahar slalom at St. Anton. Though that still wasn't good enough, I was learning to be more aggressive. At St. Anton, for example, I was a full second behind Gerhard Nenning after the first run. I had the best second run, gaining back all but .09 of a second of Nenning's lead. I was pressing so hard in that race, I broke my ski pole pushing in the flat, six gates from the end. I would have won if I could have continued to pole across the finish line.

Finally, there was my first in the Hahnenkamm slalom and combined at Kitzbühel—a victory that proved to everyone and especially to myself that I was world-class skier of the first rank. That was the breakthrough I needed to ski aggressively in every race: you can't ski at maximum speed unless you're psychologically prepared—confident of your ability and positive you can win. I followed the Hahnenkamm win with a first in slalom, a second in downhill, and a first in the combined at the Grand Prix de Megève. Next, I took a first in the giant slalom at the Alpine Countries Cup in Davos. And I ended the season with firsts in slalom and giant slalom at the Bud Werner Memorial in Vail, Colorado.

In the 1965–66 season, I really hit my stride: first in the giant slalom, downhill, and combined at the Critérium; first in the giant slalom at Adelboden; first in the Hahnenkamm slalom; first in the Megève giant slalom; first in downhill at the French Championships at Chamrousse; first in the Arlberg-Kandahar combined at Murren (entitling me to the diamond A-K pin for having placed in the top three for four years, including a first in combined); first in the U.S. Championship giant slalom at Stowe; first in slalom at Sun Valley; and, that summer, first in downhill and first in combined in the FIS World Championships at Portillo, Chile—tantamount to the crown as the world's best Alpine skier.

The Portillo victory was the most satisfying, not only because it established me as the world's champion Alpine skier, but also because it was the first major downhill I had won. The Austrians, for their part, claimed that the Portillo downhill was more like a giant slalom, and that's why I won. They were to have their chance to see whether I was really the best over a whole season, for it was in 1967 that the Evian World Cup was established. A total of seventeen races—including all the major ones—were designated as World Cup competitions with points awarded separately for each discipline. The point system has been changed several times since, but when I was competing, a skier received twenty-five World Cup points for a first, twenty for a second, fifteen for a third, eleven for a fourth, on down to one for a tenth. Over a season, the maximum you could win in any one discipline was seventy-five points. If you took firsts in three World Cup slaloms, three World Cup giant slaloms, and three World Cup downhills, the maximum you could win would be 225 points. Once you had achieved your seventy-five points in one discipline, other victories in that event would add nothing to your total, but they would still be important to stop a rival from getting a first and thereby gaining on you.

I started the season with firsts in giant slalom and combined at the Critérium and then a first in the Adelboden giant slalom. Then I had a first in the Lauberhorn downhill, slalom, and combined at Wengen. Even then, the Austrian press didn't want to concede that I could beat their racers at downhill. They were saying things like, "Oh, well, Wengen . . . that's not a real downhill. That's a wax race. Wait till the Hahnenkamm." At Kitzbühel, though, when I set a new course record in the Hahnenkamm downhill, they began to believe that Portillo was no fluke.

I remember a curious thing happening at Kitzbühel after I had won the downhill and then raced in the slalom. The Austrians are great ski fans, but they are also very partisan. When an Austrian is on the course, the crowd screams and shouts encouragement from the moment he's in the starting gate until he has crossed the finish line. When a Frenchman is racing, all you can hear is the sound of his ski edges cutting into the snow. French people who attend a race at Kitzbühel are almost afraid to cheer their racers because of the hostility of the crowd.

Thus, it was before hushed spectators that I won the first run of the slalom. Schranz, loudly cheered, of course, also had a good run and was still in a position to catch me. In the second run, he skied ahead of me and had an excellent time. Pandemonium broke loose as the spectators thought Schranz was going to win. Then, on my second run, there was absolute silence till I was about half way down the course. The announcer there is very good and gives the times all along the course, and toward the end just ticks off the seconds so the public is aware just how the race is going. Well, as it began to be obvious that my time was going to be better than Schranz's and that I was going to win by a good margin, the crowd suddenly began to yell. I couldn't understand it. And when I crossed the finish line, having won the downhill, both legs of the slalom, and the combined, the crowd was screaming and a mob of young kids broke through the cordon and headed my way.

I feared they were going to lynch me. I had beaten their

favorite, Schranz, and they just weren't going to stand for it. I looked around for help from the French team, but nobody was in a position to get to me.

Instead of stringing me up to a tree, though, the crowd hoisted me on their shoulders and marched me in triumph all the way into town. It was unheard of . . . an Austrian crowd taking a French racer to their hearts! But they are such great sportsmen that even though their idol had been beaten, they couldn't allow my performance to go unappreciated.

After that, I took: first in downhill, second in slalom, and first in combined at Megève; first in downhill at the Pre-Olympic Games in Chamrousse; first in the French Championship giant slalom; first in the Arlberg-Kandahar downhill and combined at Sestriere; first in the U. S. Championships in downhill, slalom, giant slalom, and combined at Franconia, New Hampshire; first in the Bud Werner Memorial downhill, slalom, and giant slalom; and first in the World Cup giant slalom at Vail, Colorado; and first in the Wild West giant slalom at Jackson Hole, Wyoming. I had won the World Cup in all three categories with the maximum possible score of 225! No one has done this since.

I know listing these results this way sounds like a stock market report, but without citing the record, I find it hard myself to comprehend the kind of season I had that year. No wonder I was the favorite the following year at the Grenoble Olympics. That 1967 record was as incredible as a major league baseball team's ending the season with a won-and-lost average over .800 or a hitter with a batting average over .600.

At the start of the Olympic season, though, I wasn't doing too well. Michel wanted me to take it easy, so I wouldn't peak too early. I had a first in the giant slalom at Adelboden, and then two weeks before Grenoble had a fairly good result in the Hahnenkamm—I had a second in the downhill and won the combined. Normally, I'm not much encouraged by a second, but on this occasion, I had made a very serious error on the section of the course they call the Steilhang and lost my speed through the *chemin forestier,* a long, narrow flat trail through the trees. I knew that if I hadn't made that error, I would have won, which told me I was back in shape, my skis were fast, and I was skiing very well. This was all very encouraging, but I didn't expect to win the downhill easily.

As I mentioned, Michel timed me in the nonstop and found I was a second and a half faster than anyone else. After Gerhard Nenning—who I felt was the man to beat—broke his skis, I was feeling pretty good. As an example of my positive attitude about my chances, I recall this experience: the morning of the down-hill, the weather was so bad (there was a wind and a heavy fog) that they had to postpone it. We were all sitting in the bar at the top of the Casserousse Mountain drinking red wine and eat-ing sandwiches, waiting while they kept announcing half-hour postponements. It was obvious the race wasn't going to be held that day—you couldn't see anything—and some of the guys were very jumpy. But it didn't bother me at all. By then, I was ready, calm, and confident. I went back down and had a good night's sleep, which I'm sure wasn't the case for many of the other competitors.

I must say, it wasn't easy to get a good night's sleep there. I had to ask the police to guard our chalet so the crowds wouldn't come in. There were thousands of people milling about trying to see me, to wish me luck, to get my autograph. Along the course, it was even worse: crowds such as I had never seen before at a ski race. There must have been 25,000 people watching and cheering. And cheering for me louder than for anybody else.

You may remember what happened in that downhill: despite accidentally scraping off all my wax, I won by .08 of a second. After that victory, the crowd was even more vocal. In the giant slalom, I am usually very confident for this has always been my best event. Thus when the crowd started cheering louder and louder as I was skiing down, I thought it meant they were con-vinced I was skiing fastest, which in turn just encouraged me to ski better and better. Now, as a matter of fact, they were probably not cheering that particular performance, but just my name and the fact that it was *their* Jean-Claude Killy on the course. But I didn't realize this at the time, and the cheering just spurred me on. I had broken two buckles on my boot in the starting gate, but I didn't pay any attention to that. Normally, it would have bothered me, but then I didn't care. I had safety straps on my Nevada bindings, so I just tied the thong tighter to replace the buckles. I was sure I was going to win anyway.

The first run was held under perfect conditions: a hard track under a cloudless sky. All that yelling *could* have been for the way I was skiing because I really did have a fantastic run, 1.20 seconds ahead of the field. For the second run, it was foggy again, so I skied a bit more cautiously. I was sure that with the big margin I had, no one would catch me. The American Bill Kidd, who was really out of contention after his first run, went all out and had a very good time, beating me on the second run by .08 of a second. For the two runs, I was still over two seconds ahead of my nearest challenger.

Then came the famous disputed slalom. From the outset, I knew the slalom would give me the most trouble. I was confident that I was better than anyone else in giant slalom, and after my good time in the nonstop, I was also confident in downhill, despite my wax problem. But slalom is always a gamble. There are a lot of gates and you have to ski them twice going at maximum speed, which makes for a lot of pressure. In the history of the Olympic Games, it's rare that the favorite wins at slalom. Even Toni Sailer wasn't the favorite in slalom. So I decided I would just ski it very relaxed, try my best, and see what happened.

The course for the first run was relatively simple: sixty-three gates almost straight down the fall line with very few tricky combinations. But the weather had turned foggy again, and there was a lot of talk about a possible postponement. The day before, the qualification round had been cancelled with a much lighter fog than we had for this race. But the organizers were concerned about finishing the Games on schedule, so the race was on.

I had drawn number fifteen, normally a bad starting position since the course is apt to be rutted by the time number fifteen runs. Furthermore, running first in the second run, when the field is reversed, one is apt to find the snow too soft till after a few racers have gone down the course. But on this occasion, my number was lucky for me because by the time I was in the starting gate, the fog had lifted somewhat. I had the best time for the first run: a half second ahead of the field, not exactly a comfortable lead. A lot of skiers were in a position to catch me. Only .69 of a second separated first and fourteenth place— probably the closest race in Olympic history.

The second run had sixty-nine gates, again mostly down the fall line except for a few spots where there were some severe changes of direction. One of these tight places was between gates 18 and 21, and this was to play a dramatic role in the outcome. As I said, for the second run, I was to be the first down the course; this time, the visibility was terrible. The fog had closed in, and though I tried hard to have a fast run, the weather conditions prevented me from going all out. Still, I felt pretty good as I waited at the bottom to see how the others would do. When Haakon Mjoen of Norway came down, his posted time was better than mine, but the way he fended off the reporters made me think something was wrong. He was more than a second faster than I had been, and although I felt it was possible for someone to beat me, that big a margin didn't seem possible. Sure enough, shortly afterward, word came down that he had missed gates 17 and 18 and was disqualified.

Then came Karl Schranz. His first run had been fairly close to mine, so I knew he was a threat. But when it came time for Schranz to run, he never appeared at the finish line. After about six or seven minutes, the next racer, the Swiss Dumeng Giovanoli, came through the finish line. Then, a little later, when the first seeding was almost out of the way, Schranz finally came through, having been permitted a rerun. His time was 50.02—.34 of a second faster than mine and enough for a gold medal, everyone thought. I remember my brother Mike was waiting with me and wanted to know what was going on. "There was some trouble on top," I said. "Don't make any comments to anyone. It might still turn out that Schranz will be disqualified."

I didn't panic during this waiting period. At first, everyone thought I was third. Then Mjoen was disqualified, and I was second. Daniel Petrat, an interviewer from the big television station, Europe Number One, came up to me right after the end of the first seeding and asked, "How do you feel losing that third gold medal? You had two golds and you had a big chance to catch Sailer, and you blew it. How does it feel to have missed it?"

And I said to him, "Wait a minute, the jury hasn't decided yet. I don't think they're going to allow Schranz's victory to stand."

What happened was that Schranz skied off the course between gates 19 and 21. Some observers have testified that he said nothing at first until someone suggested to him—half jokingly—that he ask for a rerun. Then he claimed that he had seen some shadowy figure on the course blocking his way. He was allowed a rerun pending the outcome of a jury ruling on his claim, and in his rerun, he had a very fast time. People have argued over whether it was a help to Schranz on his last run to have skied down half the course beforehand. I believe it was an advantage to have known about the problem posed by the gate combination where Schranz first skied off the course, but that is really irrelevant. The jury had to decide whether Schranz's claim of interference was valid or not. And it voted three to one, with one abstention, that there had been no interference. The film showed that a course policeman had indeed crossed the course just above gate 21, but in that fog, it is questionable whether Schranz could have seen him. In any event, the jury ruled that the policeman, at the moment he crossed the course, was certainly not interfering with Schranz.

A year later, I found out that Daniel Petrat, the interviewer for Europe Number One who had asked me how it felt to lose that third gold medal, had gone to see an astrologist before the Games, and his astrologist had told him I was going to win two medals, but not the third. Based on that, Petrat was certain I had lost. Yet, two hours after he interviewed me, I was declared the winner.

Those three gold medals were to change my life. Of course, I didn't realize it at the time. People have asked me whether I had considered what these victories might mean to me financially. In all honesty, I didn't think about this for a second. It isn't that I never thought of money. I've been talking about "when I turned professional," "my days as an amateur," and so forth, but it is no secret that in any pure sense, no world-class skier is an amateur.

There's no way we racers could have lived the lives we did without money. We were totally dedicated to skiing, working twenty-four hours a day at it all year round. In the summer, we traveled to the Southern Hemisphere for ski testing and additional training. All this took money. We had money from the French Ski Federation, from the Ministry of Sport, and from the pool of equipment manufacturers. That was official. But in addition, we were getting paid as individuals. Everyone on the circuit was getting paid—except maybe the Americans, and some of them, for sure, had their deals, too. From my various sources, I made about $40,000 in 1967 and again in 1968. Some of this money was permissible under Olympic rules— what they call broken-time money, for example. Some of the payments were questionable, even though permitted by the FIS— such as the contract I had with Dynamic to test their skis. Other money was strictly against FIS and Olympic regulations. For example, the French manufacturers' pool paid us prize money for first, second, and third place finishes. I think it was something like $800 for a first place in a World Cup race. But we were getting this money openly—paying taxes on it in France, for example—and the Austrians and Swiss and others were doing the same thing.

I must point out that some racers were encouraged by this situation to get greedy and pick their equipment according to the highest bidder. That wasn't my attitude. I skied for Dynamic because I thought they had the fastest skis. Dynamic at that time was a very small company; its factory was then making only about 5,000 pairs of skis a year. Such a small company couldn't afford to pay what a bigger company could have. What's more, I insisted on having what is known as an open contract—the right to ski on other brands if I felt Dynamic didn't have a model that was right for me in one of the events. And, in fact, most of the time, I was skiing on both Dynamic and Rossignol. That's why my Dynamic contract wasn't more than about $800 a month. For me, what mattered most was winning races; I didn't want to be in a position where I couldn't use the fastest skis I could find for a given race.

Nevertheless, I was clearly in violation of Olympic rules, and so were many other major competitors. We thought that Avery Brundage and the International Olympic Committee were probably aware of what was going on, but, of course, we didn't want to challenge them directly because we wanted to stay in the Olympics, which are still the biggest races in the world. And the International Olympic Committee didn't want to disqualify everyone who was taking money because to do so would have destroyed the Games.

The attraction of the Winter Olympic Games was that they assembled the world's greatest competitors—supposedly amateur competitors. But the rules about who was an amateur would have made it impossible for any world-class skier to participate. For example, before 1966 the rules stipulated that you weren't supposed to train for more than twenty-eight days. That's just stupid. If a racer could get broken-time money for only one month of skiing, that would mean only millionaires could be world-class racers. Honoré Bonnet put it accurately when he said, "The only amateur skier is Karim Aga Khan."

We all felt that what we were doing was just. After all, if you devote ten to fifteen years of your life to racing, all you know when you're through is how to race. None of us wanted to end up like punch-drunk boxers, former champions who have nothing in their later years but their memories. It seemed perfectly natural that we should make money to put aside for our non-racing days. We would not have skied if it had been otherwise.

I don't say that what we were doing was right. The whole system was wrong, and the hypocrisy extended up to the highest levels. When Karl Schranz was ousted from the Games at Sapporo, I thought that was terrible. Even though Schranz and I were never what you might call close friends, I was very sorry for him. Mr. Brundage should have known that Schranz was only doing what the top thirty skiers in the world had always done. But if he had banned the thirty best skiers, no one would care what happened in the Olympics. So he just picked on one man, a man who had worked very hard all his life to get where he was, who at age thirty had won everything except an Olympic gold medal, and who had sacrificed a normal life so that he could be in contention.

Probably, Mr. Brundage would have liked to have made the same kind of example of me at Grenoble as he made of Schranz at Sapporo, but I didn't believe he would do it. That possibility was probably the only sense in which I thought Grenoble could be a turning point in my career. From a monetary point of view, there was no comparison between my position and, let us say, that of an Olympic boxer who turns professional after winning a gold medal. Olympic boxing is considered second rate; it isn't until a boxer becomes an open professional that he can make real money. In tennis, amateurs used to make good under-the-table money, but as soon as professionals made more, open tennis, pitting amateurs against professionals, was inevitable. In skiing, we used to have the unique situation where amateurs made more money than the professionals (a situation just now in the process of changing). In 1968, there were a few professional ski races, but no one could make a living doing nothing but that. Thus, for me, there would have been no advantage in turning professional in order to receive prize money openly. At that time, there just wasn't that kind of money around. A ski professional in those days was someone like Stein Eriksen, the Norwegian Olympic gold medal winner who became a ski school director, a racer, a stunt performer, an endorser of ski and other products, a ski shop owner, and a host of other things which all together brought him an income reportedly only slightly more than I was earning as an amateur.

All this explains why money was not on my mind as I was competing at Grenoble. I didn't believe that I could make much more from skiing than I was already making. I suppose that's not quite true. I had met Mark McCormack in Geneva in July of 1967 and he had told me of his work with Arnold Palmer—work involving endorsements, modeling, personal appearances, licensing, and so forth—and even though Mark is very conservative, he mentioned figures which at that time sounded to me like an awful lot of money. But I wasn't sure that was the kind of life I wanted to lead. In particular, I didn't think I wanted to spend as much time in the United States as this sort of thing would require, so I had put Mark's proposals out of my mind.

After Grenoble, I talked with him some more, and the whole thing began to look more attractive. But I didn't want to quit racing until I had won my second World Cup. And suddenly that was in jeopardy. It was charged that *Paris Match* had paid me $7,000 for exclusive pictures of me wearing my three Olympic gold medals. Marc Hodler, the head of the FIS, suspended me, then accepted my denial and reinstated me in time to ski at the Grand Prix of Méribel for my farewell appearance in France. I won the giant slalom there, then left for the States for the last races of the World Cup series.

I had a bad weekend at Aspen, won the slalom and giant slalom at the Five Nations match at Sun Valley, and was first in the slalom at Rossland, British Columbia. I had wanted to stop after Sun Valley—I had already clinched the World Cup— but I was persuaded to go to Rossland to please the Canadian fans, and then was again prevailed upon to go to the last race of the season at Heavenly Valley, California. It was on April 8 —I remember the date well because that was the day Jimmy Clark, the Formula I driver, died. (I had done some car racing myself and was considering turning to that sport full-time.) It was while I was at Heavenly Valley that I finally decided to sign with Mark McCormack—the actual contracts were drawn up in May. Interestingly enough, in that Heavenly Valley slalom, my last as an amateur racer, the victory went to none other than my future Benson & Hedges circuit rival, Spider Sabich!

Once I signed with Mark, I was suddenly in a different world. I don't mean the cocktail parties or meeting famous people. That was nothing new to me. I myself had all the fame one could dream of. The difference was that I was leaving behind me the life of the ski racer, a very disciplined life involving hard training, constant physical effort, and, for success, total dedication. I had gone as far as I could go; there was no reason for me to continue to make the sacrifices such a life demanded. I was young, in great shape, and looking to get a little fun out of life. The first big contract McCormack negotiated for me was with Chevrolet—for an amount well up in the six-figure range. The actual amount was open, depending on how many things I did. It was a long-range deal involving many options, and, though I didn't fully realize it then, many obligations. Among the first projects was a thirteen-part TV series called "The Killy Style." These were half-hour shows that made up, in essence, an exotic travelogue: skiing a volcano in New Zealand, the ultra-steep "four walls" of Chamonix, riding horses on ice at St. Moritz—a sort of "endless winter" along the lines of the popular surfing film *The Endless Summer.*

For me, this was fantastic—not just the money, but the experience, for it took me to Australia, New Zealand, Switzerland, Italy, and France. The European places I knew intimately, of course, and I had also visited Australia and New Zealand before, but only to go to the ski areas and race down the mountains all day. Now, the work was before the TV cameras, and for me it was very relaxing. My old French teammate Léo Lacroix was along too, and as far as we were concerned, we owned the world. We could raise a little hell if we wanted to, spend as much money as we liked, and didn't have to worry about training schedules and being up for the next race. It was work too, of course, but mostly what they wanted of us was relaxed skiing for the cameras, and this was fun.

I hope I'm not giving the impression that a ski racer lives a monk's life and that suddenly I was free to fool around. For a Frenchman, an occasional glass of wine is a dietary necessity, and sex—well, a group of young, virile males could hardly be expected to stay away from the girls. Karl Schranz, I'm told, believes that sex and racing are mutually exclusive. I don't know if he really practices what he preaches, but my own feelings are different. I believe skiing and sex have a special affinity.

This has nothing to do with the reputation I acquired about that time as a sort of sex symbol—a reputation, I admit, I don't mind even though I'm not sure how I acquired it. I've always had good relations with the press. I believe in answering journalists' questions honestly and politely, and maybe these guys were just being nice to me in return. On the other hand, if a guy is not too bad looking, is a famous sports champion, is making a lot of money, is single, is generally seen with pretty girls, and has a couple of well-publicized affairs with movie actresses or an automobile company heiress, I suppose that makes him a candidate for the American newswriters' title of sex symbol. Add being the object of a paternity suit and speaking English with a French accent, and you can understand why I had it made as Mr. Sex.

But most of that was media ballyhoo. I don't claim to be made of wood, but I'm not an aspiring Casanova, either. Take that paternity suit, for instance. Every time I went to Austria, there were threats that I would be arrested because of the charges of a young Kitzbühel lady that I had fathered her child back in 1964. This went on and on for years until the Austrian court insisted that blood tests be entered in evidence. Now you can't prove paternity with a blood test, but you can disprove it. So in the presence of her lawyers and mine I gave some blood which was tested in front of all kinds of witnesses. And that was the last anyone heard of that charge.

This sort of thing is part of the disadvantages of fame. Every sports figure, I suppose, has female fans who just want to be able to say that they've made it with their idol. I remember one time early in my amateur racing career when Jimmy Heuga and I went to visit a girls' school in Vienna. Skiing, of course, is a very big sport in Austria, and the headmaster of this school had asked us to come, telling us that these girls all knew our race records and thought we were great. Well, we couldn't get out of there. They wanted to swarm all over us. We finally had to escape by a window leading onto the roof of the building, jump across to another building, and climb through another window to get out. Maybe if that story had been known, I wouldn't have been such a sex symbol. The truth was, as a racer I always had plenty of opportunities along these lines; I just couldn't take advantage of them very often.

In any event, reputations on these private matters are always a bit suspect. Once, in Sun Valley, a local guy fixed me up with a girl who, in turn, fixed me up with the kind of souvenir I could have done without. In other words, the memory of her embraces was not all that lingered from the encounter. Rather than infect anyone during the period I was on medication, I avoided intimate contact, though at that time in my life, this wasn't easy to do.

I later learned that some of the girls who consequently couldn't get as far with me as they expected to with a great French lover were spreading the story that I was gay—a homosexual. That struck me as very funny. Possibly some of them would have preferred to report they had to take penicillin because of contact with Killy than to have had their offers of favors refused.

The special affinity that I see between skiing and sex, however, has nothing to do with my own special experiences or with any of the girls who chase after ski racers. What I have in mind is the relaxed attitude one finds in the mountains and especially in ski resorts. You know, skiing is an unusual sport in the matter of dress. Skiers must get dressed up to perform their sport. It's not just a question of dressing against the cold, which they have to do, too. A skier has to put on heavy boots to control his skis; he needs goggles for vision; and he must have gloves and pants, even when it's warm, to protect against the snow's abrasiveness. In most other sports, like tennis, track, or swimming, you take *off* your clothes to perform the sport, then you get dressed again, back into street clothes. After skiing, you go back to your lodge and undress, coming out of the cold world into the warmth. You undress not only physically, but mentally and psychologically, too. You have a drink before the fire, and you feel warm and cozy and in the mood for the warmth that comes with sex.

I've met girls in Paris who seem reserved, aloof—girls who turn me off by their cold airs. Then I meet them in Val d'Isère, and they're totally different people. The same girl who is standoffish in Paris, in a completely different world will unwind—and undress. Of course, she has come there for a holiday, to relax and have fun, so it's normal that her behavior isn't the same as when she is surrounded by the pressures of everyday life. The only places I've seen with freer sexual attitudes than ski resorts are beach resorts. Much of the same thing applies there, with the additional stimulus of all that body exposure and contact.

For me, the big change in social life wasn't new temptations or new behavior patterns, but simply the possibility to relax and enjoy life more, to go to nightclubs without worrying about the next race. I must say, in the United States it wasn't always possible to do this in as relaxed a way as I would have liked. If I went to the Folies Bergères in Paris, for example, I don't think anyone would point out to the audience that I was there. They'd feel I had come for my private pleasure, and they wouldn't dream of intruding by introducing me. But if I went to a big show at Las Vegas, someone would always tip off the M.C., and I'd have to stand up and wave hello to everyone and later sign autographs. After a while, though, I got used to it, and I didn't mind.

The McCormack organization was doing its work well, and soon I found myself on a very tight schedule. For an endorsement of a product, I would be required to pose for ads (stills or videotapes), attend sales meetings, and, frequently, go on personal appearance tours. I didn't want to spend all my time in the States—I missed seeing my father and my friends at Val d'Isère—so I tried to compress all of this schedule into four or five months. In addition to my Chevrolet contract, I had signed with Eagle shirts, United Air Lines, Bristol-Myers toiletries, Evian water, *Ladies' Home Journal, Sports Illustrated, Skiing Magazine,* Breckenridge and La Daille ski resorts, and a host of ski equipment and apparel manufacturers including Head Ski, Lange boots, Mighty Mac sportswear, Wolverine gloves and after-ski boots, Look bindings, Sitski skibob, to mention a few.

My name had become what is known in merchandising circles as a "hot commodity." Had there been at the time of my Grenoble victories a viable pro racing circuit, would I have followed the same course? I don't know how to answer that. I do know I have no regrets for the way I spent the years following my retirement from racing. I couldn't have done the same thing had I continued to race; the demands on my time would have been impossible to meet. Probably, my representatives, International Merchandizing, would have recommended doing both, but on a more limited scale. Nevertheless, I might have turned this down because at that time I was looking for something different. If I had to do it all over again, the only thing I might change would be the absence from my schedule of any vigorous exercising. I came to realize how important active participation in sports is to my physical and mental well-being. I now feel it was a mistake for me to have stopped training entirely, for I'm sure I got tired a lot more easily during my personal appearances than I would have had I kept in better physical shape.

Some people interpreted my tiredness as boredom or lack of interest in what I was doing. Ever since childhood, when I had a pulmonary infection, and particularly since my army service, I've had to have more sleep than most people. But if I showed signs of fatigue or took steps to see that I had my rest, I was criticized for it. For example, I appeared in the series of fall promotional events known as the consumer ski shows. On one occasion on the West Coast, invitations were sent out for a press conference with me, and when I failed to show up, the writers attacked me in the press, saying I no longer cared about what I was doing and didn't even have the courtesy to call to say I wouldn't be there.

The real facts are somewhat different. Harry Leonard, the organizer of the ski shows, had sent a telegram to the press in San Francisco inviting them to come meet me. And he sent it out over my signature. Apparently, there was some misunderstanding about this, but I didn't know that the telegram had gone out. Harry Leonard had asked me to come to a press conference, but I thought it was just a regular press conference for the ski shows—not a meet-Jean-Claude-Killy conference—so, needing the rest, I turned him down. The contract I had wasn't very precise about this kind of obligation, and I just felt too tired to attend. I certainly didn't stay away out of boredom.

I not only had to attend the ski shows for Head and United, but also the auto shows for Chevrolet. This would involve three appearances an afternoon at the Chevrolet booth with a lot of beautiful girls. Don't get me wrong—that was a pretty good deal. I would alternate with O. J. Simpson, the football player, who was really a fantastic showman. He was quick on his feet and funny enough to have been a nightclub entertainer. For me, though, it was a lot of work, really quite wearing. Unlike Simpson, I didn't always have the right answer—mainly because my English was still a little shaky. I taught myself English with Léo Lacroix back in 1964; he and I would read to each other out of one of those phonetic language texts—I think it was called Assimil. I remember the first sentence was, "My tailor is rich." That's the equivalent of Americans learning French by saying, *"La plume de ma tante est sur la table."* (My aunt's pen is on the table.) Our sentences were spelled out in French phonetics so that "My tailor is rich" looked like this: *Maille télor iz ritche."* And the alternative would be *"Maille télor iz notte ritche."* Maybe that wasn't a very good way to learn, but as a racer, when I came to the States for maybe two or three weeks at a time, I had no trouble getting around the ski areas, hotels, and restaurants with what everyone told me was my sexy French accent. But now I was in the States for four or five months at a time, and I was really supposed to be a salesman. At the auto shows, for example, I was supposed to tell the customers how skiing was like car racing, or answer questions about ski resorts or whatever they wanted to know. While I was talking, the pretty models would be demonstrating the cars. They got a lot of attention, too, so that took some of the pressure off me.

I also went to dealers' meetings and sales meetings of company personnel—not just for Chevrolet but for most of the companies I had contracts with. I'd go to Philadelphia, say, for the general sales meetings of the Eagle shirt people, and I'd have to tell them what I was doing, what I thought of the new Eagle line, the directions in which I hoped the company would move, and things of that nature. If I were bored with this kind of work, I would not have been very effective and could not have continued to get such contracts.

No, I wasn't bored with this work. It was a new life for me, but it was what I wanted. It was my choice, and if I were faced again with the same options, I would make the same choice. I felt as though I had become a real person, not just a racing machine. I didn't even consider what this kind of life would do to my ability to race again because I was sure all that was behind me. Still, when the opportunity came to go back to racing, I looked on it as a new challenge, one that was all the more difficult because I had done so little training.

3
RELATIONSHIPS AND EXISTENCE

IT'S EARLY in the summer, a warm, clear, ideal Sunday afternoon. To get back into shape for the pro tour, I go for a workout at the Parcours Vita at Onex, just outside Geneva— it's one of these exercise courses that have been springing up all over Europe in recent years. This one has a charming shaded trail that winds through woods for about a mile or so, with twenty stops along the way. At each stop, there's a panel describing an exercise you're supposed to perform, things like chinning, situps, jumping over bars, walking back and forth on a rail, etc. I run through the course twice. When I get to the exit, there are half a dozen or so people sitting on the benches along the pathway. It's evident from their glances and whispers that I've been recognized. I quicken my pace and run toward my car. When I finally drive off, it's with a sigh of relief.

I'm not shy; I don't consider it an imposition to be asked for my autograph; yet I'm afraid of being alone in a crowd. This is not an irrational fear: I've been detained by a crowd surrounding me, and I know it can get unpleasant. I don't like to offend anyone, but some people take advantage of this kind of situation. Fame isn't all pleasure.

I'm driving over to Thonon to visit Michel and his wife Chantal. A car passes me with a teenaged girl sitting in the rear seat. Suddenly, she starts gesticulating wildly, and it's clear she recognizes me. The car slows down, and she rides kneeling on the rear seat looking out the back window, her elbows on the rear shelf, her chin resting on her hands. Every so often, she throws a kiss. I smile at her, and as her car turns off, I wave good-bye and throw her a kiss.

Though many times it can be charming, I get no special satisfaction from being recognized. No matter how often it happens to me, it's always a surprise. This isn't something I need in life, certainly nothing I've come to expect. Even when it's only the smile of a sweet young girl, it's also a bit of an intrusion. I've heard that some people, once they've tasted fame, find it's like a narcotic. They need more and more of it. For my part, I'm basically a private person. When I'm surrounded by a crowd that won't let me get away, when I'm falsely sued for paternity—at such times, I'd be happier if my name were Jean-Claude Schmidt. Even when fame brings more pleasant things, my ego doesn't crave this kind of recognition.

After Grenoble, my fame carried with it new responsibilities. When I was racing as a member of the French team, I could be rude to people who wanted to foist their attentions on me. I don't really recall ever being deliberately rude, but I never had to remind myself that I had an image to protect either. Once I had decided on a career of endorsements, public appearances, and the like, I had to sacrifice a certain amount of my private life. This wasn't necessarily a burden. In retrospect, I regard my acceptance of this state of affairs as a sign of growing maturity.

People have sometimes commented that I seem ill at ease in public. This surprises me, because in my family, I am certainly the biggest social mixer. My grandfather was a builder, a fairly successful one. He had one of the first cars in Alsace. And he was also one of the first skiers in the Vosges Mountains. I didn't know him, but I've been told he was a man with a terrible temper—the kind who would invite 150 people to a party, and then five minutes before the party was to start, go to bed saying he had changed his mind and didn't want to see anyone. And the party would go on without him. He was a very moody man.

My father, Robert Killy, is moody too, but in a different way —more like a recluse. He's a very hard worker, the kind of man who has no enemies. Everyone likes him. But he doesn't want anyone to intrude. He has a few close friends—most of them, like him, Alsatian—and all he wants is to be left alone. An evening's entertainment for him is sitting in front of his TV alone with his wife. He hates parties. He likes to meet people, but on an individual basis, not in big gatherings. I have an older sister, France, whom I don't know very well. She grew up with our grandparents after our parents were divorced when I was five years old. She's married now to Michel Mignot, the ski school director at St. Lary ski area in the Pyrenees. I can't say whether she's a very sociable person, but I know my younger brother Michel (we call him Mike) is like my father: he enjoys solitary pursuits. In him, such behavior is quite acceptable because he's an artist—a painter.

I don't take after the family in unsociability, but I'm like all the Killys in my respect for labor and the value of money. To friends of our family, that may seem paradoxical because my father's attitude toward money was peculiar in some respects. He had some very good business ideas and was always giving others advice. For example, he was one of the first to think of putting a restaurant and bar on top of a mountain, right on the ski slopes. He was convinced this would pay off and he advised a friend of his to start one. Well, that guy has a tremendous business now, and he's had lots of imitators all over the world. Still, it was my father's idea. He had lots of ideas like that, but he didn't particularly care to take advantage of them. As long as he had enough money to live comfortably, he didn't care about getting rich. What he did for us kids, though, was to teach us to work for what we wanted.

For example, I remember once I wanted to buy a fast car and I asked his advice. I had no money for it, but he said, "Go ahead and do it. You'll have to borrow money, and I know what's going to happen. You're going to have all kinds of problems. But the only way you'll find out about the troubles this car can bring you is to buy it and see for yourself."

He was right, of course. Chances are, I would have gone ahead and bought that car anyway, but having his permission gave me a sense of responsibility. His consent was a challenge to find ways of getting what I wanted, to do it on my own.

The fact that my parents broke up when I was very young had a lot to do with this sense of responsibility. They were divorced in 1949 when I was not yet six. My sister went to live with our grandparents, and my father brought up the two boys by himself. I was responsible for a lot of things at home for as long as I can remember. Maybe that's why I always felt older than other kids my age.

When my father first came to Val d'Isère, he had a ski rental shop, which wasn't a very big business then. Later he managed a ski shop in town and then moved into his own ski shop. Then he also opened a restaurant, and when business got better, he bought a hotel. Now he has a hotel and two ski shops, one of them run by my brother who spends his winters in Val and his summers in Normandy or Brittany, where he finds the colors ideal for painting. The hotel is run by my stepmother. My father remarried in 1955 to a very wonderful woman. But by that time, I was already away at boarding school, so in effect, my attitudes toward life were formed entirely under my father's influence.

This includes my attitudes toward sports, for my father had been an excellent ski jumper and a good Alpine skier, too, though he had to give it up after he badly smashed his leg in an accident. And, I suppose, my parents' breakup was at least an unconscious influence in my attitudes toward women. Woman was for me an object, something to be taken. I had no interest in establishing a close relationship with any girl. It could very well be that my feelings were related to my mother having left us. As I grew older and began to have affairs with girls, I found I couldn't stay with any one woman for more than two or three days at a time. I was not only very mistrustful of women, I just had no respect for them at all. This applied to my attitude toward women ski racers, too—I never thought ski racing was a sport for women, and frankly, I still don't think so. Later, when I began to have more mature feelings, I loved a woman for being a woman. All I wanted from her was just that—to be a woman. Nothing more than physical contact. After my father remarried, these attitudes started to soften, not only because Renée, his wife, is such a fine person, but also because her daughter, my stepsister Audrey, moved into the house, and we had a more normal family life. By this time, though, for much of the year I was either away at school or away skiing or training. Still, my father wanted to keep the family together, and we have been very close. I never did get to know my sister France very well. After she married and moved to the Pyrenees, I saw her even less frequently. But my stepsister grew up in our house, and now she lives in Geneva, so we still see a lot of each other. She's married to the European manager for the Lange boot company, Roger Micol.

The biggest change in my attitude toward women, of course, came when I met my fiancée, Danièle Gaubert. That was on New Year's Eve, December 31, 1968. She had come down to Val d'Isère to relax after finishing a movie. She dropped into this nightclub that belonged to some friends of mine, a place I used to go to all the time to play poker.

Two weeks before, her picture had been on the cover of *Paris Match* in connection with a review of her latest picture— I think it was *Les Régates de San Francisco* (The San Francisco Regattas). I recognized her from that picture and so I was pleased to see she was with someone I knew, an Iranian girl named Manon. And Manon brought her over to my table to introduce her.

I remember I was holding two low pairs, and when I looked up at Danièle, I reached for the wrong stack of chips and bet more heavily than I would have on such a hand. That bluffed out the other players—nobody saw me—and I won the hand. That was sort of a good omen, and I smiled in appreciation at Danièle, who struck me then, as she does now, as a very beautiful woman.

watching me play cards for some time—not the most entertaining way to pass a vacation evening. Finally, I stood up and we went to the bar and had a drink. I made a date to have lunch with her the next day at the Solaise Restaurant up on the mountain. She had just taken up skiing—she was on short skis and was doing very well, able to go anywhere. I didn't ski with her, of course, but we really hit it off.

After all the beautiful women I had been going with, suddenly here was one who was not just an object for me, but a real person. Danièle had been divorced about two years at that time—she had been married to Leonidas Rhadames Trujillo, son of the Dominican Republic dictator. We found we had a lot of interests in common—she's quite a sports enthusiast, for example, and has become a very fine skier. We liked doing everything together.

I had to go to the States shortly after we met and didn't see her again till March. She was down in the Bahamas—she was making a movie on Grand Paradise Island—and I arranged to spend some time with her there, visiting her on her sets. It was when I took the time out of my very busy schedule and spent all that money to visit her that I realized how much she meant to me. I knew this was it.

Later, she came to the States to be with me on my tours and on the Killy Challenge, and our relationship deepened from passion to the true love of mutual respect and enjoyment of one another. We have been together now for four years, and I expect we'll get married one of these days.* But the truth is, neither of us is very anxious to formalize our relationship that way. My feeling is that unmarried couples tend to have a continued courtship without ever taking each other for granted. You get married and then you don't shave every day or she stops putting on makeup. That's personal, of course. The right guy and girl will work things out together married or not. But Danièle and I feel that things are just fine now, so why change things, even though, for the sake of her kids, we'll probably formalize things later. She had two children with

* That day occurred on November 2, 1973, as this book was going to press.

Trujillo—Marie Danièle, age eight, and Rhadames, age six—who live in Paris with Danièle's mother. I confess, it's possible that my attitude toward marriage is still influenced by my childhood experience of seeing my parents divorced. And maybe Danièle still feels hurt from her first marriage. I gather it was quite stormy. They were from two different worlds—he a young millionaire who spoke only Spanish, she familiar only with the relaxed atmosphere of the French film world. It didn't work out. He remarried and now lives in Spain. I've never met him, though he visits with the children every year or so.

In any event, we're living our lives as we like—not to challenge anyone's code of ethics or to revolt against existing mores, but simply because this particular mode of life expresses our private feelings at this stage in our careers.

My meeting Danièle led to other changes in my life. Through her, I became interested in the movies as a career, I broadened my circle of friends to include people from the arts and theater, and you might also say I refined my sensibilities through absorbing some of her perceptions as a woman. I don't mean that she completely changed my tastes. For example, I have always had a hard time reading a novel. When I know something didn't really happen, I can't relate to it. My favorite author is still Saint-Exupéry and his genre of writing. Personal exploits artfully told remains the kind of book I enjoy most, while Danièle prefers a novel or even a book of poetry. But she did make me aware of a world that had been almost totally alien to me before.

I don't want to make it sound as though Danièle is a jet-setter or that her concerns are those of a social snob. On the contrary, she's most happy as a homemaker, taking pride in her cuisine, her table arrangements, the furnishings in our house. We both prefer a quiet evening with friends chatting over a glass of wine to meeting people who are famous. Some famous people, of course, are impressive, but what impresses me isn't their fame. When I met General Charles de Gaulle at l'Hôtel Matignon in Paris . . . well, *there* was an impressive man. This was right after my victory at Portillo, and he said, "M. Killy,

I saw your performance on television. You skied admirably—a credit to the sport and to France. I'm confident you'll continue to serve your country well." He was a very tall man, and I had to look up at him, and all I could say was, *"Oui, mon général."* You know, it's like talking to history. He gave Frenchmen a feeling they were independent, that they had a responsibility as Frenchmen. He thought athletes were good ambassadors for the country, and he saw to it that a good deal of money was spent on sports. And that's why he gave me the Legion of Honor, France's highest distinction: because he felt it was important to associate my victories with the grandeur of France.

I never sought out famous people just to meet someone who was well-known. I'm equally impressed by someone who has achieved excellence even if he is unknown. A fine furniture maker, for example, is a king in his own world, and I admire that. In my scale of values, a Louis Pasteur is no more admirable than a Bernard Palisy, the sixteenth-century potter who burned his furniture to cook ceramics. If I do admire Pasteur, it's not because of his achievement, which, of course, was tremendous. What I admire in him was his dedication. He was doing what he liked, was totally involved in it, and made personal sacrifices to continue his research. That he discovered many things that were important to the human race is almost incidental. I have the same admiration for a mason who keeps building houses because that's what he likes to do. In short, dedication, the total involvement in any undertaking—and that's what I had in ski racing—is what is very special to me, what is really important in life.

If I had any disappointment in the life I was leading after retiring from ski racing, it was in not being allowed to dedicate myself as fully as I thought I would be expected to in some of my contracts. For example, what I know best is the design of skis and ski boots. I had contracts with Head skis and Lange boots, and I expected to help conceive these products, to help test them, to help make them the best on the market. That's not what happened.

This may not have been anyone's fault, exactly. Michel Arpin was also hired by Head, and the Head people had tremendous respect for him. I had suggested they hire him because I knew that he understood me, and if I found some way I thought a ski could be better, he would know how to translate my opinions to the factory. That's how we used to work at Dynamic. Michel was then still working at Dynamic, but at my suggestion, he left and went with Head, as we both thought we'd have better opportunities with a large company to get what we wanted in the way of product improvement.

But it didn't work out. Though some of the Head principals had a lot of respect for Michel and for what we wanted to do, others were shocked at some of our proposals. We didn't realize that a big assembly line is not like a tiny factory that produces virtually handmade skis. At Dynamic, we'd go into the factory and talk to the guys making the skis and stop what they were doing and tell them what we wanted—and we'd get it. That's why we had the best skis in the world at that time. But two Frenchman can't go in and change a whole American assembly line. The Head plant was set up to produce metal skis. They were very good metal skis, but we felt the future was in fiberglass skis. You can't attempt to revolutionize a whole production line without upsetting a lot of people in the plant. We didn't know that at first, but it soon became apparent that Head, with the best will in the world, just wasn't going to produce the kind of skis we thought they needed.

As I've said, the contracts I had were very lucrative. My income for the period between when I went with McCormack to when I went back to racing was in seven figures. But I couldn't just take my money and run. As I mentioned, I didn't simply sign a contract with General Motors and walk off with hundreds of thousands of dollars. It was a long-term deal with an option for so much if I made this TV series, another option for so much if I went to the auto shows, and so forth. To the public, it may have seemed that I was laughing all the way to the bank, but no one gets that kind of money without producing. In point of fact, I probably netted more than that announced figure from all the work I did for Chevrolet, but this was over several years and included many separate contracts. The point is, I worked hard and in general there was mutual satisfaction with the arrangements.

Head was the major exception. We might have worked things out, but Head changed ownership. We had to deal with a succession of different people who never did understand what Michel and I really had to offer them. With all the knowledge that the two of us had, Head should have been able to use us to great advantage, but they didn't.

There were problems with some of the other products I had endorsed, too, though of a very different nature. Bob Lange of Lange Boots, for example, simply wanted to have the world's best skier under contract. He came down to New Zealand while I was filming "The Killy Style" to convince me it would be a good idea. Later, there was no attempt to get any feedback from me about what I thought a boot should do. The truth is, Bob Lange never had any plan about what to do with me once I was under contract. He saw nothing wrong with paying me just for my name, for my endorsement. I was in that business, of course, but I expected a difference between endorsing a product only for the promotional value of my name—products about which I had no special knowledge— and endorsing products like ski boots, about which I could be expected to have something worthwhile to say.

The skibob presented a different problem. Though it was a very good product, it was simply ahead of its time. A skibob is a kind of bicycle on skis, with handlebars, a seat, and small skis that the skibobber wears. Anyone can learn to skibob in a day, and it's lots of fun. It's become very popular in Europe and in some parts of the States, but at the time I endorsed this skibob, it was still a new sport.

Another mistake was the Wolverine contract. Wolverine is a big shoe company that wanted to get into the ski business. The principals thought my name could help them, and they put it on a line of after-ski boots they bought in France. Unfortunately, the boots were not very fashionable and were too expensive. It was my fault, in part. I should have said that these were not the kind of boots I wanted to have associated with my name. But at that time, I was not very experienced in business and didn't foresee the consequences. Financially, it worked out well enough for me because Wolverine bought back the contract. And I suppose it worked out for them, too, because they did get into the ski business and are now the American distributors of Rossignol Skis and Le Trappeur Boots.

I mention these difficulties not because they were typical but rather because they were the sole exceptions to a generally smooth business career. Mark McCormack's organization knew the kind of things I wanted to do, and mostly I was involved in work I liked. They never suggested an endorsement for a liquor or cigarette company, for example, because they knew I would refuse. Though my work didn't involve total dedication, for the most part, I enjoyed what I had to do to fulfill my contractual obligations. Not everything, of course: I didn't enjoy working in a studio, posing for still photography. I knew I had to do it sometimes, and I did the best I could. Just the same, putting on makeup and standing around waiting for some guy to tell me to smile—this I hated. Unfortunately, at first there was a lot of this kind of thing because every contract I had included using my picture for ads.

I didn't mind it so much out on the slopes. At least, there I felt in my element, and I could be more natural and relaxed for the camera. In a studio, it felt artificial, and even when I made commercials where I seemed to be relaxed, I wasn't. It wasn't a question of being camera-shy. I had been interviewed plenty of times on TV as a ski racer. But being a star on TV for your own program, reading lines in English, is a very different thing from being interviewed as a ski racer in Europe.

It was probably inevitable that I should gravitate from making TV films to making a movie, though I don't think I would have considered it if it hadn't been for Danièle. As it turned out, it was the most enjoyable experience of my post-racing life.

I had had a lot of movie offers, such as playing a French

racing driver at Indianapolis in a film that starred Paul New-
man or playing a Canadian cowboy in the film *Billy Silent*. I
turned them all down, though, because I just wasn't interested.
The *Snow Job* script sounded more like something I could
relate to, and I.M.C. talked to Warner Bros. about it. At the
time, I was out in Sun Valley making a one-hour TV special
with the Olympic figure skating star, Peggy Fleming. This was
a great show filmed by the Bob Banners Co. of Los Angeles.
They had me on short skis skating around on the ice with Peggy
—it was a lot of fun to do and to watch, and the show, which
was seen twice on prime time, later won three awards.

Anyway, while I was at Sun Valley, George England, the
director, came to visit me to talk about a picture. We had
dinner and got along very well.

"I'm not an actor," I told him. "So if I make a picture, I
don't want you to put me in situations where I would have
to pretend to be what I'm not." I knew that an actor is supposed to be able to laugh or cry or change his personality as
the script demanded.

George England assured me the script wouldn't require me
to try anything I couldn't handle. "You'll just have to be yourself," he promised, "and do a little skiing." That sounded too
easy, so I wasn't convinced. Then Warner Bros. sent a plane
to pick me up—it was Frank Sinatra's private plane, I believe—
and took me to meet John Kelly, the president of Warner's.
Both he and England reassured me and explained what they
expected of me.

For my part, I pointed out to them what difficulties they
would run into filming on a glacier. They agreed to provide
a helicopter and promised to get any other equipment we might
need. Danièle was along, and they told me they wanted her to
play the female lead, which made me feel more at ease about
the whole project.

We had lunch with the Warner executives. All this attention
had the anticipated effect: they made me feel so important and
made it all sound so easy, I decided to sign the contract.

We went on location to Cervinia, a ski resort on the Italian side of the Matterhorn. We were there for fourteen weeks with a Hollywood crew of thirty to forty guys. I was well paid and treated like a star, and it was just fantastic. I don't particularly like people fawning over me, but to experience the attentions a movie star gets is a whole new world, and I figured that once in my life it wouldn't spoil me. When I had talked with England about it beforehand, I had expected the work to be much the same as I had done on a TV special for Chevrolet, but that wasn't the case at all.

Actually, that TV program had been something of a mixup. Originally, it was supposed to show me turning from ski racing to car racing. When we were almost through with it, Chevrolet said, "No way." The script had me driving a Corvette around Le Mans—testing it in the States, and then going to Le Mans to race. But in the middle of the shooting, Chevrolet changed its mind about having me as a car racer. They were hoping I would be helpful to them in selling the whole youth market, not just the sports car market. Besides, Chevrolet was not involved in racing.

As a result of their decision, we had to rewrite the script. Originally, it was supposed to end at Le Mans, which would have been realistic because I was then very much interested in getting into car racing. Instead, they had me going to Hollywood, looking around the sets there, and talking about a movie career. That turned out to be kind of prophetic, but it didn't reflect my thinking at that time. At that point, I really had no interest in the movies. I just wanted to race cars.

When I finally did make a movie, I found it was done with far greater preparation than working on a TV program. George England was far more demanding than anyone I had worked with on TV. I had no idea there could be so much pressure in acting out a single scene. Whether making a TV film or one to be shown in theaters, you know there may be millions who will see the finished product. But there's a much bigger crew watching you for the movies, and you really have the feeling you're on stage. If Danièle hadn't been there, I don't think I could have done it.

In the film, I play the part of a ski instructor who is more like a ski bum than most instructors I know. I'm supposed to have an American girl friend, played by Danièle—her voice was dubbed to hide her French accent—and another American friend who is a skimobile expert. The plot calls for us to pull off a big robbery, then hide the loot up on the mountain through a series of daredevil acts like riding on top of the cable car, jumping off, and skiing down a glacier through crevasses. The plot is a bit thin because there doesn't seem to be any logical reason for this showy stunt work, but it was written to show me doing some fancy, dangerous-looking skiing. The plot thickens when a suave insurance inspector arrives to investigate. This part was played by Vittorio De Sica, and he was just incredible. He's a man well over seventy who lives a busy life in Rome. And here he comes up to the high altitudes, works for ten to twelve hours a day, all with that special Italian class—the gestures, talk, brilliance of a general. Then, suddenly, he would say, "Mr. Director, I'm tired. I must stop." Of course, everyone would stop—we were all dead by then, anyway. And De Sica would go back to his room, shave and change, come out looking fifteen years younger, and go to the Casino and gamble all night. He was simply unbelievable.

Anyway, in the film, he turns out to be a crook himself who finds the crevasse where we had buried the loot and makes off with it in a helicopter. My friends and I are dejected at having pulled off what seemed to be the perfect robbery, only to be swindled ourselves, and I sadly bid good-bye to my American girl friend. In the last scene, I'm seen riding with De Sica in a train, indicating I was in cahoots with him all the time. That explains why we called the picture *Snow Job*.

I thought it was a pretty good movie. I admit I'm no actor, but I think if we had had more time and preparation—if I had taken acting lessons, for example—it could have been even better. Mostly, I think the problem was with the script. The lines were not terribly believable. But I don't think I need to apologize for my performance. Some movie critics had kind words for me, a few didn't. That's to be expected. The fact is that I enjoyed the experience enormously and wish I could do it again. I've had a few proposals along these lines, but I won't do it without the right script. And, of course, I'd have to have the time. Still, I expect to do more in the world of cinema.

This book is about my attempt at a racing comeback, and here I am spending pages explaining how good I had it after giving up racing. If I've spent so much time writing about my successes, it's to make it clear that I didn't go back to competition because I was at the end of my rope, that I was leading an arid existence, that racing was really all I knew and all I could do. That simply wasn't the case at all.

But there *was* something missing in my life, though I wasn't consciously aware of it at the time. I suppose you could call it a specific goal that I could work toward in the same way that I had worked toward winning consistently at skiing. I met many Americans who seemed to be able to do this in their lives, and I greatly admired them. People like Carol Shelby and Dan Gurney, the former automobile racers who had started from scratch, so to speak, and had become millionaires. There were some Frenchmen who were like them, but very few. Henri Oreiller, a ski champion from Val d'Isère, was supposed to have been something like that. I can't say he was exactly my boyhood hero because he was too much before my time, but I had heard of his exploits. He was successful at skiing and in business and later in car racing, too. Unfortunately, he was killed in a car accident while he was still very young. Jacques Anquetil, the bicycle champion, is the current French sports figure I admire most. He was always very independent: he would say what he thought and do what he wanted to. He made a lot of money from his sport, but he was completely open about it. There was no false idealism about him—he was very good at what he did and he let everyone know it. The Tour de France bike race is the kind of setting I enjoy. It takes good organization, smart tactics, knowing how to handle the other racers on your team, plus physical effort and endurance—with tangible financial rewards all along the way. Jacques

Anquetil won it five times. If I had been a bike racer instead of a ski racer, I could see myself doing what Jacques Anquetil accomplished. In other words, if bike racing had been my sport, Jacques Anquetil is the kind of man I'd have liked to have been.

In ski racing, I really had no such heroes. I was only fifteen when Honoré Bonnet had me train with the French A team, and of course, I was very impressed, especially with guys like Henri Duvillard, Guy Périllat, and Léo Lacroix. I didn't regard them so much as heroes, but as guys whose technique I could copy. I would watch the faster ones, particularly Duvillard because he was a downhill specialist and I wanted to be good in downhill, but even at age fifteen, I told myself that, as good as these racers were, I could be better. So I regarded them less as people to emulate than as racers I could learn from and eventually surpass.

I met Carol Shelby while I was still a ski racer. In 1967, I drove around his racing course in Riverside, California. I was impressed by him as a teacher as well as by the kind of friendly, outgoing person I found him to be. He helped me understand what the United States was all about. I don't mean by giving me lessons in history, but just by being a person I could relate to.

This was even truer of Dan Gurney, another great racing car driver. If you asked me what an American is, I'd think of someone who looks like Dan Gurney: very tall, good-looking, relaxed, walking around in tennis shoes with his hands in his pockets. And yet, he builds beautiful cars and was one of the best drivers in the world. I went to visit his place in Santa Anna and watched him testing cars at Riverside and I saw that this man knew what he wanted to achieve. His workshop didn't look like a mechanic's bench—it looked like a surgeon's operating room. He knew cars, knew how to make them go fast, and knew how to build them to go faster still. His current interests and achievements are a continuation of his life as a racer.

Though I had some interest in turning to car racing, I realized that it was too late for me to achieve in this field what I had achieved in skiing. Carol Shelby had told me I was a natural, that my reflexes, my sense of line, and my ability to memorize a course—all of which I had from skiing—were great assets for car racing. I had a few good results in some car races I entered, but these didn't tempt me into fooling myself; I knew it wasn't possible to start all over again. Besides, I felt responsible to my family; car racing is quite a risk if one engages in it as a regular activity.

Still, Dan Gurney had a very strong influence on me—in the same way, perhaps, as reading about Abraham Lincoln might have on some kids. I met other men who were highly successful —men such as Edwin Cole, the president of General Motors. When you realize that you're talking to someone who has 100,000 people working for him, you have the feeling that you're in the presence of more power than most human beings have, more even than some heads of state have. Someone responsible. And yet, when we had dinner together, I found he could talk about anything. And he could go home after work and play with the kids and their electric trains. John Delorian, another GM official, was the same type. Yet, these men didn't impress me in the same way that Dan Gurney did because success in itself is not what I admire most. What I admire is tenacity, struggle, and dedication.

Perhaps I can make this distinction clear by citing the careers of two race car drivers, François Cévert and Henri Pescarolo. I've watched them over the years; they were similar in many respects—both very talented. But Cévert, before he was killed at Watkins Glen in the fall of 1973, had achieved fame and rewards. Pescarolo, on the other hand, has never really made it big—at least, his remuneration has seldom been commensurate with the effort he puts out. But he keeps working, keeps trying, keeps making the sacrifices. He's the kind of person I admire most—not the guy who is most successful.

My admiration is even greater, of course, when I see someone like Gurney, who had both the rewards and the dedication. I can't say I envied Gurney—envy isn't the right word because I certainly had no conscious feeling of missing something that he had. But in retrospect I can see that I was missing his sense of dedication. It would have made sense for my life to be more of a continuum, building logically on the base I already had.

I don't know if I can explain this adequately. The athlete, when he puts away the tools of his trade, can have a tough time adjusting. His fame will usually open any door he wants. He can talk directly to the top man, and his immediate opportunities are enormous. He can get any kind of job—but can he hold it? I'm sure if I told somebody I wanted to sell stocks, I could find a stockbroker who would hire me. But if I didn't have the background or aptitude for this, what good would it do me? I could knock on the boss's door and start at the top, but in two months I'd be out. The ordinary guy might not get to see the boss, but he'd start at the bottom and learn his trade and eventually be a success. The problem is, the athlete whose name is a household word might find it very difficult to spend those necessary years of apprenticeship, working as an unknown after years of fame.

In my case, I was cashing in on my fame as an athlete, working hard at it to be sure, but without a specific goal in mind that could involve all my concentrated energy. I'm naturally aggressive, and that certainly is an asset in business. But I have to be hooked—really committed to something. Otherwise I don't care and I don't try. The big problem for the athlete in the nonsports world is to find a cause he can set his energies to that will involve him as he was involved in his years of competition.

Sometimes, the conflict in making this transition is so severe, the delicate mechanism of the brain is affected. This happened to François Bonlieu, an Olympic medalist who could not adjust and who spent time in a mental institution before dying in an accident in Cannes in August 1973. True, François showed signs of imbalance even as an amateur racer receiving the plaudits of the public. Nevertheless, I'm convinced he would not have suffered such a breakdown afterward if it weren't for this conflict between the life of the sports champion and that of the retired sports figure abandoned to his fate.

Needless to say, my own condition could not be described as having been abandoned to my fate. Such was not the nature of my malaise. I was the highest paid ski racer in the history of the sport, perhaps one of the most financially successful athletes in any sport. And I was good at what I was doing—promotion and public relations. The missing link was a long-range sense of purpose in what I was doing. That's hard to retain when day-in and day-out you answer the same questions.

"Jean-Claude, when did you start racing?" "What do you think of American ski resorts?" "Which is your favorite ski area?" "What do you think of American women?" "How do you have the courage to go so fast?" "At what age should I start my kid skiing?" "Which are better, metal or fiberglass skis?" "Which is the safest ski binding?" . . . "Jean-Claude, how can you stand answering these same questions over and over again?"

Yes, I get asked all these questions repeatedly—including that last question. It's terribly tiresome, and frankly, just to amuse myself, sometimes I make up answers which are not exactly the ones I believe to be true. But when I get tired of answering the same questions, I'll stop and think a bit, and I'll remember things like the time I met Arnold Palmer. We were having dinner at Maxim's in Tokyo, and though I knew the kind of questions he must get asked, I couldn't stop myself from doing the same thing, posing really stupid queries such as, "Is it better to concentrate on the ball or on my swing?" I'm sure that's the last thing in the world he wanted to talk about that night, but I still couldn't stop myself. I knew I would take advantage of what he told me and go out and practice whatever he advised me to do. I must admit, he was very nice about it.

Well, whenever I begin to feel exasperated at someone's asking me a question I've answered perhaps a thousand times, I remember that helpless urge I had to ask Arnold Palmer the same kind of thing. And so, tiring though it may be, I try to give a polite and helpful answer.

On the other hand, there's always that guy who's driven

100 miles just to ask, "Jean-Claude, when I'm on a steep icy slope trying to make tight turns, do I have to keep my weight all the way forward, or can I risk jetting my skis?" Now, there may be fifty other people waiting around to ask a question, but as I see this guy responding to what I say, as I see he really understands and he really loves skiing as much as I do, I'll end up giving him a forty-five-minute lesson. He's the kind of guy who has a subscription to *Skiing Magazine* and knows the top race results for the last five years, and he knows I have something to tell him. Well, there's just no way I won't talk to him. I mean, I respect this kind of guy; I *like* to talk to him, and it makes it all worthwhile to see his eyes light up as I say the one thing that clarifies something about skiing that's been bothering him, something that he hadn't understood before. After talking with someone like that, I'd feel really good, even though fifty people who had been waiting to get a word with me may have left disappointed.

One question I used to be asked frequently was, "Jean-Claude, don't you miss not skiing?" And I would answer in all honesty, "No." First of all, I had been skiing since I could remember, and unlike the city dweller who can't get enough of the sport, I had always been able to ski all I wanted to. Some racers, once they stop skiing competitively, never go back to the slopes. Guy Périllat, for example, was glad to put away his skis. If he never skied again, I don't think it would bother him a bit. I didn't feel that way at all, and even at my busiest, I had plenty of time on snow compared to the average weekend skier. For instance, my various commercials frequently required that I be photographed while skiing. And in the summer I was testing skis and other equipment. It wasn't as though I had been taken away from the mountains and forbidden to go back. Remember, for seven months of the year, at least, I was living in Geneva. My choice of the world's best ski slopes was never more than an hour or two away.

Yet, when I answered that I didn't miss skiing, I wasn't even thinking that I still skied a lot. I just meant that I had made my choice, that all of my ski racing past was behind me, and that what I had wasn't bad at all. As I've mentioned, I can't say what I would have done had Mark McCormack said to me that first year, "Look, Jean-Claude, we think it's in your best interest to race again." The question never arose because there was no format that could have made this possible. The way I felt at the time, though, I'm inclined to think I would have taken a lot of persuading. I know now there was something missing in my life, something that would have made it more fulfilling—but you never could have told me then that a return to ski racing was it.

4
HANDICAP RACING

BY THE TIME I had been away from ski racing for a year, I felt completely divorced from it. Except for Michel Arpin and Léo Lacroix, I was completely out of touch with my old ski-team friends. I not only didn't know the results from race to race, I didn't even know the names of the competitors. For example, the first time I ever heard of Bernhard Russi, the Swiss downhill specialist, was when he won the World Cup. Michel, who was following the American team on the race circuit for Head, would tell me about how good Gustavo Thoeni or some other racers were, but just hearing about it meant very little to me. Later on, I saw them at the Critérium de la Première Neige at Val d'Isère and realized how *very* good they were.

Initially, though, I had no interest. Frankly, I thought I was so much better than the other skiers, there was no point in my getting involved. I suppose that's why I really wasn't interested in professional racing either. It's been suggested to me that even if pro racing at that time was strictly minor league, if I had become involved, that in itself would have made it a big-time sport. I don't think that's true because you can't sustain spectator interest if one competitor is head and shoulders above everybody else, and at that time, I was sure there was no one around, amateur or professional, who could come close to me.

During this period, Mark McCormack was giving this whole question a lot of thought. He believed that my business position would be stronger if I were an active sports figure rather than a retired one. One of the ideas Mark had was to put together a three-way contest: Karl Schranz, Bill Kidd, and me. Mark told me that the thing that had made golf a success on television was the three-way contest among Arnold Palmer, Jack Nicklaus, and Gary Player. He thought a Schranz–Kidd–Killy contest could do the same for skiing but he was never able to arrange it. He was sure, though, that professional skiing could never be a success until a format could be devised that would make it work for TV.

Then one day he said to me, "Jean-Claude, I've got it. If there wouldn't be any contest pitting you against any other skier around today, all we have to do is give your opponents a handicap."

Mark was no skier, and I just figured he didn't know what he was talking about. "That's crazy," I told him. "What do you want me to do, ski with a forty-pound pack on my back?" I was thinking of the extra weight a horse has to carry in a handicap race.

"No, no," Mark said. "I mean giving your opponents an advantage, as we do in golf."

At that time, I didn't know anything about golf or how a golf handicap system worked, so I asked him to explain.

"In golf, if a player has a five handicap, let's say, it means that at the end of eighteen holes, he deducts five strokes from his score. A zero-handicap player would have to beat him by more than five strokes to win."

"That's ridiculous. You can't have anything like that in skiing. How would you work it? I never heard of any such thing."

"Why shouldn't it work?" Mark wanted to know. "You could simply give the other guy X number of seconds handicap, and then you'd have to beat him by that much to win."

We had already discussed how one racer running after the other, each against the clock, as they do it in amateur racing, was a poor format for the spectator, particularly on TV, and I reminded Mark that his idea would put us right back into that situation.

"Not at all," he argued. "You could give the other guy a five-yard lead or you could just leave the starting gate after he does. Then you've got your handicap and still you'd have a head-to-head dual slalom."

"That's ridiculous," I kept insisting. "Leave the gate after the other guy? I never heard of anything so foolish."

But it wasn't so foolish, and as I thought about it, I realized Mark was right. We could develop a lot of drama this way. If I lost, it wouldn't damage me, because the handicap was simply a way of getting a lesser skier to ski with me on even terms. So Mark started to pull it together. He got United Air Lines and Hertz Rent-a-Car to sponsor it. We called it "The Killy Challenge," and what we decided to do was to tour around at different areas—ones served by United and Hertz, of course—and at each place, a group of four racers would compete against one another in eliminations, with the winner challenging me for $10,000. We weren't quite sure how to determine what the handicap would be nor how we would apply it on the course, so initially I remained sceptical.

Another problem was that when the series was ready to be launched, I was just getting off the ski show tour and I really hadn't done any training at all. Initially, it was hard for me to build up any enthusiasm because this was being done strictly for film. The only spectators around were the people who happened to be at the area at the time plus those connected with putting on the show. Doug Pfeiffer of *Skiing Magazine* set up the courses and provided technical commentary for the TV announcer, Gil Stratton. Doug had a tough job trying to set up courses that were identical or nearly so. Not only did the gate combinations have to be set exactly alike, but the contours of each slope had to be manicured to resemble one another. Otherwise, the handicap would not have been meaningful.

Before we started the series, Jay Michaels of Trans World International, the Los Angeles film company that was doing the photographing, came up with the idea of using Christmas tree lights for the start—the kind they use in drag car racing. Each racer has a bunch of lights in front of him. They'd flash red, red, red; yellow, yellow, yellow; and then green—and you'd go on green. They'd have these electronically timed so that my green would flash on the precise number of handicap seconds after my opponent's green flashed on. The concept was just fabulous—it really made me a believer. Until I saw those Christmas tree starts, I still didn't have much faith that the handicap system could work.

Setting the handicap was something else. The first idea we had was to have Léo Lacroix act as pacesetter. The difference between the other racers' times and Léo's would then be the handicap. This was something like the way our Chamois de France races worked and the way the American NASTAR ski races work today. The only trouble was that Léo was primarily a downhill specialist. Too many of the other pros were able to beat him in slalom, which, of course, meant that his time could hardly be used to set the handicap. For the first race, held at Snowmass near Aspen, Colorado, we just gave everybody an arbitrary half-second handicap.

The finalist in the four-way competition was Christian Pravda, an old-time Austrian champion who had become a ski instructor, perennial professional racer, and anything else he could do to earn a living while skiing. Pravda had neither the finesse nor the showmanship of his old rival Stein Eriksen, nor the business acumen of his countryman Othmar Schneider, nor the perpetual youthful exuberance of still another Austrian, Anderl Molterer. But like them, Pravda was a former star who loved skiing and was still fiercely proud. He didn't want to be beaten with a handicap, but he didn't think he could beat me with only a half-second lead. So on the one hand, he bragged that he would give me a half-second handicap, and on the other, he insisted he should have a full-second handicap. After all, he argued, I was only twenty-six and he was in his forties.

The truth was, Pravda had been skiing every day and was in great shape, while I had been on the ski show tour and had only ten days on the snow with no real training beforehand. But I told the sponsors that I would go along with the full-second handicap. Well, Pravda raced very well and just narrowly missed beating me with what we thought was a full-second handicap. But then it turned out no one had told the timers about the change. Pravda had actually had only a half-second handicap. Had he been given the full second, he probably would have won. He demanded a rerun, and there was no choice but to give it to him. This time, he had his full second, but I bore down much harder and beat him by a larger margin than I had in the first race.

After this, we decided that the best way to set the handicap was to have me run the course all out and then compare my time to the best time the challenger had registered during the eliminations. At first, there were some complaints that I might not try hard enough on my handicap run, but after a moment's reflection, everyone realized I couldn't risk not having a better time than the challenger's. And it was soon obvious that the handicap represented a fairly accurate measure of skiing ability. For example, at Squaw Valley, the elimination was among four women racers. In tennis, Bobby Riggs recently made headline news by challenging women players, but when I did it women's lib had not yet become such a big thing, and nothing much was made of my racing against the girls. It turned out, this was my toughest race because the handicap I gave was enormous— 3.2 seconds.

My challenger was Cathy Nagel, a former U.S. Olympic team member. You have to remember that most ski races are won by hundredths of seconds, and here I was waiting in the gate for 3.2 seconds before I started off after this Olympic-caliber skier. It seemed to me she was halfway down the mountain. In the first run of the slalom, my binding released at the top of the course, so I lost that run. In the next run, I beat her. In the format we were using, the best two out of three won. That meant that if one course was faster than the other, the racer on the faster course in the runoff would have the advantage. To make it as nearly fair as possible, therefore, we would have a toss, and the winner could have his choice. Well, against Cathy, I won the toss, but under the circumstances, how could a gallant Frenchman do anything else than give her the choice? And she beat me. To win the $10,000, though, she would also have to beat me in giant slalom. But I won that, which meant we had to have a runoff. That went three runs, too, and in the deciding run, Cathy had the faster lane and took full advantage of her big handicap. By the time I left the gate, I was sure I could never catch her. I probably couldn't have, either, except that she fell under the pressure.

There were some other close calls on that tour. At Jackson Hole, Wyoming, the winner of the challenger's round was Hermann Goellner, an Austrian ski instructor I had never heard of. He had never been on the Austrian A team, so I assumed he couldn't be much of a racer. Later, I learned he was quite a stunt skier, having won the first exhibition skiing contest that Chevrolet and *Skiing Magazine* put on. But at that time, his name meant nothing to me. Was I in for a surprise!

Hermann was one of those diminutive, rosy-cheeked Austrians, but in the way he skied he was most unlike the other Austrians I faced on the Killy Challenge. A quiet, unassuming guy, he skied with what some people were beginning to call the Killy style. His handicap was the minimum—a half second or something like that. And he adjusted very quickly to the format —better than most of the others I met on that series. He forced me to a runoff, and I thought he was going to take me. He was strong enough to race me on even terms, without the half second handicap. Only lack of experience beat him. I guess Hermann had noticed that I picked up a lot of time in the starting gate. I was used to the Christmas tree lights, first from drag racing, and also from skiing this format more than my challengers. But Hermann caught on to the way they worked so that he, too, could prepare himself to shoot out the instant the light went green. In the runoff, though, he got overanxious and jumped the gun twice in a row. The rules stated that three such infractions would disqualify you, so on the third attempt, Hermann was overly cautious; thus we started out almost together. Even so, he led all the way down. I caught him in the last gate, and the only way I did was by noting a bump right near the finish line and launching myself into the air to pick up a precious fraction of a second.

It's funny, at the outset of the series, United and Hertz were afraid I would lose and spoil the attraction of the series that way. But after I kept winning, they hinted they wouldn't mind my losing once just so the series wouldn't look rigged. I figured if someone could beat me, fine; it would be good for the series. But I just can't go out to race and not try to win. There were actually some whispers that the guys let me win, that I paid them not to beat me. I could have done that, of course, because I certainly had the money for it. It would have cost me more than the $10,000 prize money each guy could get by beating me, but let's assume I was willing to pay it. You don't race against guys like Christian Pravda, Stein Eriksen, or Pepi Stiegler and even hint at their throwing a race. These men are all former Olympic champions with tremendous pride, and it would not have been possible to buy them. As for myself, well, I can't picture myself paying someone to let me win. It's not in my nature; it's alien to the sport; and it would be insane. Presumably, one would do such a thing to improve one's image. But that sort of thing gets out—it's bound to. Rather than helping his image, the skier would be creating his own Watergate.

No, the Killy Challenge was very much on the up-and-up. Perhaps the best proof of how hardly fought these races were is the case of my contest with Pepi Stiegler at Sun Valley. Stiegler was an Olympic gold medal winner in giant slalom who had become the ski school director at Jackson Hole, Wyoming. A superb skier who was on the slopes all year round, Pepi had never let himself get out of shape. He doesn't drink or fool around, he just likes to ski—and he skis well. I knew I was in for a hard time when I made my handicap run because I went all out and still only barely managed to beat Pepi's time.

Though these races were being run primarily for the TV crews, in this case considerable local interest was generated. There were a lot of Austrians at the Sun Valley ski school at that time, and a whole bunch of Pepi's friends were there to root for him. I had my friends, too, and the situation created a lot of feeling. As long as I can remember, the Austrians have been France's archenemies in skiing. It was like that way back in the thirties, too. Nobody can win all the time, and it would be no disgrace to lose to a skier like Stiegler. Along with

Goellner, he was certainly the best of my opponents that season. Still, if I had to lose, I would rather have lost to Léo Lacroix or Michel Arpin or Pierre Stamos.

I suppose it's strange I should feel that way, coming from an Alsatian family. Alsace, for a period, had been taken over by Germany, and many Alsatians speak German. In Val d'Isère, there was some feeling among the rest of the population that my father and his Alsatian friends were outsiders. We were called *les Chinois,* the Chinese, which means coming from another part of France; but in Val d'Isère, all the "Chinese" were Alsatians. There was M. Charles Diebolt, who invented giant slalom poles and the Chamois de France. The mayor, Dr. Petri, was Alsatian, M. Louis Erny, the head of the sports club—all my father's best friends—were also Alsatians. My father spoke German as a schoolboy—I don't think he could speak French till he was six or so, and even today, he speaks German as well as he does French. If history had been different, I would have grown up German-speaking.

But as it is, I don't speak a single word of German. I must say, today, I'm a bit ashamed of this, but when I taught myself English, it never occurred to me I could gain anything by learning to speak German. When I was a young child, the Germans were still considered the enemy we had been fighting during the war. I knew people like Michel Arpin's father-in-law, Jean Talon, who had been in the Nazi concentration camps because he had fought against Franco in Spain. To this day, anything German is anathema to him. And as I grew older, the German-speaking skiers—the Austrians, Swiss, and Germans—were still our enemies. We were very jingoistic on the French ski team, and I guess I am still very nationalistic in the sense of having a special emotional response about being French. After all, as a competitor, I had been taught that I was a representative of my country. Initially, a racer represents only himself. Then, as he wins, his family takes pride. For me, it was always very important that I was pleasing my father with my victories. Then it grew to pleasing my towns-people—winning for Val d'Isère. I was very proud that there were more ski medals in Val d'Isère than anywhere else in the

world except Kitzbühel. At Innsbruck, I wore the French uniform, met the Minister of Sports, and got the feeling I was
on a special mission for my country. This feeling increased at
Portillo for the World Championships, and at Grenoble, on
French soil, I could say it was part of me, in my blood.

I respected many of the Austrian skiers, of course. I learned
a lot watching Egon Zimmermann II, and one couldn't help
admire Karl Schranz for the fighter he was, though I was never
friends with him. Outside the French team, in fact, the only
close friend I had among ski racers was the American, Jimmy
Heuga. Naturally, when Jimmy did well, I was pleased for
him, but that was a strictly personal reaction. I was happy
when a Frenchman won even if I didn't like him personally.

I suppose that these strong national feelings are not good
for the Olympic ideal. The Games are supposed to pit individual
against individual. But the IOC doesn't run the Games that
way. And frankly, I think the national feelings *ought* to be part
of it. For me, much of the excitement at an Olympics is seeing
which country comes off with the most medals. I admit, the
Olympics have become too big, too commercial, and too
political. Clearly, the reason the politicians want to get into
the act is because there's so much publicity and advertising.
They know the exposure will be good. I think that's why the
Palestinians came to Munich. In my view, though, the only
thing wrong is the size. If the Games were small, reserved
for sports lovers and team members, there could still be a
healthy expression of national feelings without things getting
out of hand.

In any event, right or wrong, Stiegler and I both grew up
in an atmosphere where a race between us couldn't be just a
race between two individuals named Stiegler and Killy. It was
bound to include the aspect that he was Austrian and I was
French and by the same token was bound to take on something
of the nature of a grudge match. Given that background, it
couldn't have been more dramatic. Both slalom and giant slalom
went to three runs, with each scoring a victory, so we had to
have a runoff. Though the couple of hundredths of a second
handicap that Pepi had didn't seem like much to the spectators,

I remember coming out of the gate knowing that Pepi already had a lead and that I had to chase him all the way down. For me, waiting in the gate even for that split second was agonizing because getting a fast start has always been one of my strong points. Try as I would, I couldn't seem to gain enough on him to overtake him. As we came to the finish line, though, I thought I might be almost even so I shot my legs out to break the finish line light beam. The red light flashed up on my course indicating I had won. Paul McCollister, the owner of the Jackson Hole ski area, where Pepi worked, came running over screaming something like, "The light was wrong. Pepi won. We were robbed. Pepi was first! We all saw it."

The films showed that Pepi's upper body had indeed crossed the finish line before mine. But my skis had crossed first. No doubt, Pepi hadn't realized that the electric eye was that close to the ground. Whenever I study a course before a race, I always check to see where the finish line beam is, just in case I have to rely on it to win the race. This was one of those cases, but it was not cheating. I simply took advantage of a situation to gain another fraction of a second. Without the handicap I had given Pepi, that wouldn't have been necessary. But I'm sure Pepi's supporters remain convinced to this day that I won only through some sort of skulduggery.

I had one other close call in this series, and that was against Stefan Kaelin, a former member of the Swiss team. This was at Park City, Utah, one of the few places where the two courses were grossly unequal. Stefan was able to beat me when I had the slower lane. In the runoff, though, I was able to take him.

The American skiers I faced were no problem. They were good skiers, but their forte was trick skiing, not racing, and at that time, the hot-dog contests had not yet come into vogue. Guys like Tom LeRoi and Bill Paterson were great showmen, though, and the TV people gave them a lot of exposure, which they liked very much.

There was something very appealing about these American skiers. Racing wasn't a big thing for them, though some of them were very talented and probably could have been good racers with the right training. I'm talking not just about the guys I competed against on the Killy Challenge, but about a host of really good skiers I met at all the top areas. They wear Levis and sleep in trucks and eat hamburgers, but they show up on the slopes with the best equipment they can buy. They'll join the ski patrol or wash dishes or do anything around a ski area that will keep them alive and let them go skiing because that's what they love to do.

I remember a fellow I met in Aspen named Bob Chamberlain. He earned his living from photography, but he was really an artist and one of the world's greatest powder skiers. For him, powder skiing was his life; it was an art form. He and others like him were responsible for the development of new skis made especially for powder, and you could almost say they developed a special technique for powder, too. Bob had long hair and not very much money, but when he was in deep, untracked snow, he was a king.

When I raced, I never had much opportunity to ski powder— that is, to ski deep, unpacked snow. Races are always held on packed courses since loose, soft snow is much slower. Guys such as Bob Chamberlain taught me a lot about skiing powder, and I loved it. The first couple of times I tried it, I was on stiff slalom skis which don't work well in soft snow. *Ski Magazine,* perhaps because I wrote for their competitor, *Skiing,* took great delight in publishing a picture of me skiing badly in deep snow on those slalom skis. But once I got the right equipment, I learned how to handle the powder well, and now, I, too, love to see my tracks after my skis have carved graceful curves through a fresh field of virgin snow.

I would have lots of fun on the slopes with these hot skiers that I met at every area because I could relate to their feelings for the sport. But I didn't have to save up $200 to buy a pair of skis and then work hard for another couple of weeks eating nothing but hamburgers till I had enough to buy a pair of boots. My life was quite different: I could stay at the best hotels, travel to any ski area in the world, and enjoy myself at the level of the good skier and the tourist, too. People who saw me having fun on the slopes during this period would sometimes make comments like, "Poor Jean-Claude. If only he didn't think he had to make money, he could spend his time skiing with the people he really likes."

People who thought this were mistaken. It's true, I felt better during the eight weeks of the Killy Challenge because I *do* feel most at home at a ski area. My physical shape improved during this period, and that did a lot for my mental outlook, too. I knew what I was doing was furthering my career; so much the better if, at the same time, it permitted me to have fun.

But the choice was mine, and it was deliberate. Nobody ever told me I had to sign personal appearance contracts. Perhaps I didn't fully understand the extent to which the contracts I signed after Grenoble would be governing my life for the next five years, but I did know I was making long-term commitments, and I was prepared for it. The people who were criticizing me never had the choice. It was easy for them to say I was selling out because the uncommitted life of the ski bum was the only option they had. I was able to opt for the best of both worlds.

I think some of the talk about how unhappy I was in my new role stemmed from the reputation I had as an amateur of being a prankster. I had to have fun when I was racing, I can't deny that. To me, skiing has always been more than just running gates. I wanted to do more on the snow than simply go fast, so sometimes this led to capers like my jumping over a mound of snow and dropping my pants mid-air. A crazy piece of youthful exuberance. Everybody laughed, the papers wrote about it, and so I had the reputation of being a cut-up, a blasé don't-give-a-damn type of person. At age eighteen or twenty-two, that was probably true. If I felt like sleeping under a bridge, I'd go do it. If at age twenty-five or twenty-six, I no longer felt like that, it wasn't because I was no longer *free* to act that way. I chose a more responsible approach to life because that's me too. Real freedom is having the choice. And in my view, the guy who chooses to think and act at age thirty just as he did at age eighteen shows signs of arrested development.

So I have some advice for my ski bum friends who keep worrying about "poor Jean-Claude." Don't shed any tears for me. Keep having fun on the slopes. I'll see you there and have fun with you. Afterward, we'll say good-bye. I know what your lives are like—remember, I've been there. If I choose another way, it's with open eyes. Poor Jean-Claude? Ridiculous!

The eight weeks of the Killy Challenge were really very happy for me. Danièle was along, I was skiing every day and I was winning. Not only was the exercise good for me, but I felt that I was where I belonged—in the snow rather than out of place in a New York studio. Unfortunately, Mark couldn't find a sponsor the following year. There are a number of reasons for this. The series had been run strictly for television, and that has some built-in problems. To get a good picture, you really have to wait for the sun and for the right conditions. But United and Hertz wanted us to race at different areas, and we had a deadline schedule to meet, so that meant we had to race whether the conditions were right for TV or not. The logistics of getting to the various areas and preparing the courses meant we had no latitude. Consequently, some of the films were not as good as they should have been. Then, too, there was the problem that we hadn't attracted the young skiers, the ones who were winning in the amateurs. As a result, we couldn't interest anyone to buy the idea for a second year.

So that was the end of my racing, and this time I really thought it was for good. It just didn't seem possible that I would go back to it. For the long-range, I was thinking in terms of developing ski areas or getting into manufacturing ski equipment. The eight races I had during the Killy Challenge made for an interesting interlude in the pursuit of my career. But when Mark told me he couldn't sell the series for another season, I felt, "Well, that's that." And with only a trace of regret, I turned back with renewed enthusiasm to this other life of endorsements, consulting, public appearances, and later, to my budding career in the cinema.

5
BACK ON THE
CIRCUIT

IT'S SIX in the morning and the sun is just beginning to come up over the mountains. As the sky lights up, the colors are reflected in the waters of Lake Geneva. I take my racing bike off the hook where it is hanging in the garage. It is a fine, lightweight, ten-speed bike, the kind with the sew-up tires that have to be pumped up every day. Jacques Anquetil, the bike racer who won the Tour de France five times, gave it to me himself; it carries his brand name. Today, I plan over fifty miles, climbing several mountain peaks, so I pump hard to make sure my tires will roll well. As I pedal along the road, the only people I see are a few yachtmen tinkering around their sailboats. Further along, I pass a few hikers headed for the mountains. Otherwise, the streets are deserted, and as I get out into the countryside, I have the feeling that nobody else exists. The world is there for me, and as I cycle on, everything happening around me seems specially put there by nature for my private enjoyment. And to challenge me. When I get to the foot of a mountain, the road sign indicating the distance to the summit seems to call out, "Jean-Claude, can you get all the way to the top without stopping?" I answer, "Yes," and I'm off at full speed.

When I was racing as an amateur, I took it for granted that I had to be in good physical shape to win. I ran, cycled, lifted weights, practiced yoga, did everything the French team trainers said was necessary. I don't recall ever really enjoying the training, though. I did what I had to, and when I stopped racing I was relieved that I wouldn't be required to follow this kind of schedule any more. I had a bit of on-snow training before the Killy Challenge, but none of the other conditioning that I formerly considered essential. In the summer of 1972, when Michel persuaded me to attempt a comeback, I really think I dreaded the chore of whipping myself back into shape. And was I ever out of shape! The first day I started cycling again, I was huffing and puffing after only a few kilometers. I saw immediately how much work I had to do. But what surprised me was the fantastic pleasure I now took in working up a sweat, setting little goals for myself, and then reaching and surpassing them. I rediscovered that the pleasures I get from sports are the most intense life has to offer me.

I didn't go about my training haphazardly. I had the help of a good friend of mine in Geneva, Roland Sidler, a former Swiss bike champion who is now a professor of physical education. He worked out a careful program of running, cycling, weight lifting, calisthenics, stretching exercises—all designed to get me back into shape to ski. I started on July 18, doing just a little bit that day. On the 19th, I biked for ten kilometers; on the 22nd, I went to an athletic club in Geneva to lift weights; on the 28th, I went seventy kilometers on my bike. I would have a workout every two or three days, at first, because I was coming back from far away and Roland didn't want me to overdo it at the outset. It's funny, when I started back into training, I wasn't feeling well—I had stomach problems, I was irritable, and my weight was down. As soon as I began working out, I felt better. My stomach problems went away, and inside myself I was more at ease. I realized I had been very foolish to give up training. Even if I wasn't skiing competitively, for my own health I should have stayed in shape. I know men in their forties and fifties who continue to run and bike, and these men stay young and have a positive outlook on life. I don't ever expect to let myself get run down again.

Despite my poor shape, I didn't think I had to push myself too hard. I felt I could ski well even if I wasn't in top shape.

For example, in the spring of 1969, there was a French ski instructors' rally at Val d'Isère and the whole French team was there. The instructors raced against the ski team members to see how well they could do. And I was persuaded to race, also. Though I was completely out of shape, coming there directly from the auto shows in New York and a spring of the dinner party and cocktail circuit, I beat everybody except Jean-Noël Augert, and I lost to him by only a tenth of a second.

But that was only for one run, not a whole season, and I was then twenty-five, not going on twenty-nine. So I thought it best to follow Roland's program and to watch my diet. Instead of eating meat twice a day, I now had it two or three times a week, and without any sauces. I had more vegetables, more cereals, more fruits—in other words, more of the carbohydrates necessary for muscular effort. I had to build up my weight and replace soft tissue with hard muscles, and that takes a combination of exercise and diet. I have never believed in complicated diets, preferring to keep things as simple as possible.

I remember having dinner in Paris at La Colombe with Mark McCormack, his wife Nancy, Danièle, and Gary Player. Gary and I had both ordered very simple meals which led to a discussion about diets. Just then, the waitress brought out salads with French dressing. Gary returned his and the waitress brought it back with a plain oil and vinegar dressing. Again Gary returned it. Finally, she brought it back plain, which is the way he ate it. "Stay close to nature," was Gary's advice, "and you'll stay good longer." Basically, I share his attitude toward food.

By the time I was ready to get back on my skis, I had cycled 1,200 kilometers, lifted ninety-six tons, and run sixty-four kilometers (that wasn't quite enough running, and I was to pay for that later on). I had done something like five hours of interval training calisthenics, which consists of a minute and a half of very hard exercising followed by ten seconds of rest, repeating this several times. To do that for a total of five hours is a lot of work. My cycling also included interval training. I would pedal very fast for two kilometers, slow down for 500 meters, then fast again for two kilometers, and so forth up to

65 kilometers a day. That would be the equivalent of 170 kilometers of regular cycling. I also played a lot of squash and golf, so by the end of the summer, I felt I was in excellent shape.

In all this time, I still hadn't been on snow—except for one brief experience down in Argentina. I had been asked there to consult on the feasibility of building a new ski area, but when I got there, I realized the only way I could look over the mountain the promoters had in mind was from a helicopter. Unfortunately, there were no helicopters available for private use; they all belonged to the Argentine army.

So we asked the army if we could borrow one. The officer I spoke to was very gracious and agreed to let us have a helicopter—provided I would agree to give some ski lessons to the Argentine army ski troops. "Fine," I said. "I'll be glad to give some lessons in French racing technique wherever you say." So they set a time and place and I arranged to have a friend, Jacques Pitte from Val d'Isère, who taught skiing at Bariloche, meet me to translate what I would say into Spanish.

We had agreed to meet on one of the slopes at Bariloche, but when we got there, no ski troops were in sight. Finally, after waiting a long time, we saw a bunch of uniformed guys loading on the lift. We had told their officer we would wait for them right in the middle of the slope, so we just continued to stand there. After fifteen or twenty minutes, we couldn't figure out where they could be. We were right smack in the middle of the slope, and there was no way they could have skied by without our seeing them.

Then, suddenly there they were, swarming over the crest of the hill like Indians in a Wild West movie. We had chosen a fairly steep slope as the best place to demonstrate racing technique. Nobody had explained to me that these guys weren't ready for that kind of lesson. Many of them were on skis for the first time and all of them were trying to show off for me. As a result, they were falling into each other, coming out of their bindings, and even coming out of their boots, which were too big for them. It was unbelievable seeing them in their stocking feet tumbling down the mountain.

There I was, prepared to give racing tips to a bunch of

pretty good skiers, and the Argentine army showed up on its stomach. I laughed so hard, I actually fell over in the snow. It was a beautiful sight, really: the panorama from Bariloche is lovely—an impressive range of mountain peaks and this pretty lake. Snow everywhere. And then the army rolling down the hill. Some ski troops! I finally made up something on the spot—I'd never taught beginners before. Actually, Jacques Pitte told me what to say and everybody ended up happy. They got their ski lessons and we got our helicopter. But that brief experience was about all the skiing I did that summer.

As I've mentioned, when I started on this regime, I thought I would be involved in open racing with Thoeni, Augert, Russi, and the other amateurs as well as pros like Schranz. When the European ski federations shot us down, you can see why I felt I had to race somewhere. A lot of work and a lot of commitment, as well as a lot of time, would have been wasted. Incidentally, I kept at my training even when it looked as though it *would* all be in vain. But when I heard the Beattie circuit was going to include all those young racers in addition to the regular old pros, I knew all this effort, all this sweat, all this struggling with my body was going to be put to use.

By October I was into a heavy schedule, working out every day and watching the snow reports for some indication that we could start skiing. By this time I was down in Val d'Isère biking every day up to the Col de l'Iseran. There's skiing all year round up there on the glacier and at the Grande Motte above Tignes, but it wasn't ideal for setting gates and particularly for doing the kind of free skiing Michel felt I needed. Snow was late arriving in the 1972–73 season, so finally, we went up to the Col de l'Iseran to ski anyway—it was November 9, as I recall. I knew I had to run a lot of gates before I'd be ready to race. I still hadn't worked out a contract with any equipment manufacturer, so I didn't have skis or boots. To train, I just took a pair of skis out of Michel's shop, which was all right as a way to start but was not a way I could win races.

Two things are involved in the choice of equipment: getting the skis, boots, bindings, and poles that would give me the best chance of winning, and getting a contract with a manufacturer to use his product exclusively. I mentioned that in my last years as an amateur, I earned about $40,000 a year from the manufacturers whose equipment I used. The amateurs today probably make more than twice that amount. (I use the word *amateur* to distinguish those competing for the World Cup and Olympic medals from the professionals openly competing for cash prizes, but of course, it should be clear by now that I don't mean at all what Avery Brundage means by the word.) If manufacturers are willing to pay a man so much for skiing on their equipment when the rules prohibit their using that racer's picture or name in their advertising, obviously, they should be willing to pay even more to a professional whose name can be openly promoted and who would be willing to make personal appearances in their behalf. At least, that's what I thought, and what many manufacturers are now saying to the ski federations when the amateurs come to them for money. But as I indicated earlier, it wasn't what they said to me back in the fall of 1972.

I went first to my old love Dynamic, where Michel and I felt we would be warmly received. They practically threw us out. Rossignol, as I've mentioned, was interested in using my name for its professional team but not in having me race. In boots, there was a different problem. When I had last raced, the plastic boots were just coming into vogue. Afterward, I had a contract with the American boot company, Lange, one of the pioneer producers of plastic boots, but I wasn't using them for racing. I don't really like to race in boots that are too high or with too much forward lean. So I was looking for a boot that had the shape I like—a close fitting shell, cut low as modern boots go, permitting me to use my muscles when I want to sit back or go forward, rather than forcing me into one position. I tried Caber boots and Heschung boots and Le Trappeur, and I didn't like any of them, though I probably didn't give any of them enough of a chance. Later, I went back to Le Trappeur and discovered what a really fine boot it is. But first I tried skiing on San Marco boots, which didn't work too well for me. San Marco is Italian for St. Mark, and when Michel told me, "These are not the boots for you," I answered. "Maybe if I wear these boots, St. Mark will bless me and I'll ski like a lion and get a good result." As everyone knows, the lion is St. Mark's symbol. When I finally got a fit with the Trappeurs and decided I'd like to use them, I went to the Trappeur factory and told the owner, Jean Tricard, that I liked his boots and wanted to have a contract to race in them.

"Are you going to win?" he asked.

"Yes, I think so," I said because I really felt I would.

"I'll take your word for it," he said, and gave me a contract.

But back in November, I had no equipment contracts and really didn't have any idea of how the Beattie circuit worked. The first race was to be in Aspen on November 25, which meant I'd have to leave about November 21 if I wanted to ski there. To tell the truth, we hadn't even decided how many races we were going to enter, let alone which race would be our first. We knew very little about what was involved. Since I wasn't skiing well yet, I didn't mind if I missed the first couple of races. It didn't worry me that I wasn't back on my skis right away. That was inevitable. I expected that in a few days, things would begin clicking. I remember it used to take me very little time after a summer's layoff to get back on my skis. In two or three days, I'd have my reflexes back. Some other racers would need two or three weeks. Léo Lacroix, for example, always needed several weeks to get it all together. Guy Périllat would have even more difficulty. Guy was not a natural athlete. He was technically perhaps the best skier there ever was, a very studied, precise style. But he had to work very hard because he wasn't strong or well coordinated. Bill Kidd, the American skier, was something like this, I understand, though of course he never had the same success over the course of a season as Guy Périllat did.

So my first task when I went up to the Col de l'Iseran to ski was just to get my feet back in my boots, as we French say. The first day, I skied in the morning only, taking about twenty Poma rides. The second day, I felt my coordination returning, and I took about twenty-five rides in three-and-a-half hours, running about 125 gates. I was using a combination metal and fiberglass ski that didn't seem to be right for slalom. Or maybe it was just me.

The third day, it was cloudy and snowing at Val, so we went up to Tignes to ski the Grande Motte. It was great powder snow, and we just went free skiing, making about ten runs. Then we ran into the pro team from Rossignol, and we discussed with them whether we'd be able to train together. We had heard they were there, and we had been told they had courses with jumps on them. These guys knew the pro format and we didn't, so we figured it would help to see how they were setting up their courses.

The next couple of days, it was windy and snowing on the mountain, raining down at Val. We met with Adrien Duvillard, who was there to train the Rossignol team, and he told us about the jumps that were part of the Beattie slaloms. The Rossignol team had indeed constructed courses with such jumps on them and Duvillard invited us to try them out. But the weather interfered and in the meantime the Rossignol team left. It wasn't till the afternoon of the 15th that I got back on skis, but not to ski slalom. Instead, I made about eight long runs.

"You're skiing beautifully," Michel told me. "Your old rhythm is coming back. But I'd like to see you free skiing for another four or five days before you try to run slalom gates again. The ones with jumps in them will throw you if you don't have your balance back."

I did go free skiing again the next day—in very flat light, which made for a good test of balance and was more physically exhausting than a run in good light would have been. But time was running out, so on the 17th, we ran some more gates. Two other pro racers were there: Pascal Jugy and Peter Duncan, a Canadian. We found the bumps that the Rossignol guys had used, but fresh snow had covered them over so they weren't of much use. I was skiing faster than the others, so that was an encouragement. But I still wasn't satisfied with my equipment. I knew that the previous year's pro champ, Spider Sabich, skied on K2, an American ski, so I contacted Chuck Ferries whom I had known when we were both amateur racers and I asked him to send me some K2s to test. But they hadn't arrived yet. Meantime, I continued to try different boots. If a boot hurts, you can't ski; you've got to go to the shop and fix it. So I kept losing more time.

On the 18th, it was snowing heavily again, and all I could do was have a bit of free skiing around Val d'Isère, the weather having closed down the gondola at Tignes. On the 19th, though, I again was able to try running through gates with built-in bumps. It wasn't a good test of what we'd see later because these bumps, too, had been covered over with fresh snow.

It snowed again on the 20th, so all I could do was take a few runs in very heavy snow. On the 21st, we left for Denver. In effect, I had put in eight days of skiing, and not really a single one of those was a full day of concentrated training. I should have been skiing since early October, but I wasn't ready for it physically, and I was still trying to negotiate some equipment contracts. When I finally did get on skis, I still had no contract—I didn't even have an idea of which gear would be best for me. Thus, when I left for Aspen, it wasn't at all with the intention of skiing there. Before getting on the plane, I had a press conference in which I announced I probably would return to skiing on December 2 at Vail. I wasn't even sure of that, but at that point, it seemed possible. At Aspen, I simply wanted to see how things worked. I figured I would continue my training there and maybe come to some conclusions about my equipment problems, too.

On the 22nd, after staying at the Denver Inn, we flew by Aspen Airways to Aspen. Beattie had arranged a press conference at the Denver airport, and I think someone announced I would ski at Aspen, but I didn't consider that a commitment. At that point, I really didn't expect to race till Vail. This feeling was reinforced that afternoon when we went to Snowmass to try out our new K2 skis. We found them difficult to maneuver, especially for small correcting movements. Chuck Ferries and Gordie Eaton of the K2 Company worked with us trying to correct these problems, and I must say, they were very cooperative. I have to admit, I wasn't skiing well enough to know for sure whether the problems were with the skis or with me, but I knew for sure I didn't like them. We tried a slightly shorter pair—204 cm instead of 207 cm—and found these were more maneuverable. We tried several more pairs in the next couple of days, but we weren't completely happy with the way any of them responded.

I have the habit of saying "we" about testing my skis and training. When I listen to Michel talking about my races, he'll also say "we," especially when he's describing some error I made. "Coming through the middle part of the course, *we* got on our inside edges too much," he'll say. And as you see, I'm the same way. My skiing really is a team effort with Michel. I want to make clear that I don't use that "we" because some newspapermen used to call me King Killy. It's neither the royal *we* nor the editorial *we* I'm using here, but the literal *we* to refer to the joint efforts that Michel and I expended at every moment of the pro tour. When I fall, he feels responsible. When the skis aren't sharpened properly, we both feel at fault—there's that much involvement. Before a race, I sleep better than Michel does. Whether I signed with K2 or Rossignol or whomever, I knew that at some point Michel would see to it that I had the right skis. He was capable of going to the factory and making them himself if he had to. I wouldn't have attempted a comeback without him.

Aspen was a familiar haunt for Michel and me. We have many old friends there, like Jean-Paul Jallifier, a former racer from Alpe d'Huez who now has a ski shop in Aspen. I stayed at the chalet of another old friend, Jean Eymère, who used to live near Val d'Isère and who now runs a lodge in town. Jean was a ski instructor before his eyes started to fail him; today he is totally blind. He still skis, though; in fact, he teaches other blind people to ski—some of whom have never been on snow before. He's very successful with them. And no wonder. He inspires them because he himself is one of those people who overcame adversity by refusing to let anything stand in the way of their positive approach to life. I skied with Jean just after the races. He would ski ahead and I would follow, explaining what the terrain was like ahead of us, how many turns he could make, what dangers he had to watch out for, etc. He would go in front and make the exact number of turns I said he should. If he would head too far off in one direction or another, I'd call out for him to go back to the left or right. He got a great deal of pleasure out of our time on the slopes together—and so did I.

Jean is about thirty-five, blind because of diabetes. The loss of sight, of course, affected his whole life. "My main regret," he told me, "is not being able to see the kids." But he won't give up on life. His morale is unbelievable. A marvelous man.

Aspen is a free and easy town where no one stands on ceremony. Still, I wasn't prepared for this casual approach to extend to the races. Michel and I arrived at 9:30 the morning before the qualification runs. We wanted to watch the racers compete for the last ten places—what they call the cut. But nothing was happening. The slalom course wasn't even set up. On the World Cup circuit, the course is set up the night before, and there's a good deal of protocol to make you feel that something important is taking place. Here, ten minutes before the race, they suddenly set it up, everybody took one look and was ready to race. I was shocked. At that point, I thought the pro circuit was going to turn out to be some kind of circus rather than an honest-to-goodness series of races.

But then, seeing all the timing equipment, the gates being set up, the racers putting on their bibs, the manufacturers' reps in their vans waxing skis, filing edges, foaming boots, when I saw all that, my pulse quickened. Without even understanding what was happening, I was being drawn in. At the Denver airport, when Beattie had announced I was going to race, I didn't feel at all involved. I thought, "Good, if that helps build interest, let him say so. I'll see how things go." Now, in the middle of all those race preparations, suddenly I felt I wanted to enter. I had to be in it.

Michel didn't agree. I had had only three more days on skis at Aspen before the race and I still didn't have the skis or boots I liked. Michel thought it would be best if we remained on the sidelines, just watching the way these pro races are run. What changed our minds definitively, though, was studying the scoring system. If you do no better than qualify, it's worth five points and $225. If you get into the quarterfinals, that's seven points and $500. If you make it to the semifinals, you get a crack at the championship round, worth $2,500 and twenty-five points to the winner and $1,500 and twenty points to the runner-up. The winner of the consolation round takes third for fifteen points and $1,200, and fourth place earns ten points and $1,000.

If it was only a question of the money, I probably would not have raced. It was worth more to me to make my return appearance a dramatic one. And I knew I was not skiing well enough to provide any drama other than my own poor showing. But then I got to thinking, "Suppose at the end of the season, you lose the Grand Prix for the most aggregate points by only five or ten points? Won't you kick yourself for not having entered at Aspen?" To ask the question was to answer it. I realized I couldn't afford *not* to race at Aspen.

The way things work, there are forty racers entitled to enter each qualifying round. Thirty of these places go to the top money winners plus any FIS or Olympic medal winners—so I was automatically eligible for the qualifying round. Otherwise I would have had to compete in a preliminary, a run against the clock with the ten fastest getting into the qualifying round. They call this the cut, and it was watching this that got me upset about the slipshod way things were organized.

When I got to race myself, it was a funny feeling. Some of the journalists wrote that I seemed to have trouble with the mechanized starting gate. As I've mentioned, this is more like the stall at a horse race than the start of a ski race, and in the first few races, the system they had for opening the gate was such that if you could guess when it would be opened—or if you were in cahoots with the starter—you could get quite an advantage. But I didn't realize this at the time. I really wasn't bothered by the gate itself. The truth is, I felt out of place. I stood there waiting for the signal to be given, and I didn't know what I was doing there. Ski racing, yes, this had been my business, but now that I was back in it, I had this strange feeling that I didn't really belong there. I saw all those gates in front of me and knew I had to ski fast through them, to knock against the poles to make the shortest line I could, but I didn't have a fighting spirit as I started out. I wasn't a contender. And the results revealed my attitude. Of the sixteen who qualified, I had the worst time. I just barely made it into the opening round.

My skis were no help. I used the 204-cm K2s and broke the edges on my first run. I may have hit a rock, because the snow cover wasn't too good. The race was supposed to be held down at Little Nell at the base of the lifts, where the maximum number of spectators could watch. But there wasn't enough snow, so it was moved up to Tourtelotte Park in front of the restaurant at mid-station.

In the second run, I used the 207-cm K2s, the ones I had so much trouble with when I tested them at Snowmass. Small wonder I didn't get past the opening round. Nevertheless, it was worth five points to me, and it was precisely to pick up a possible five points that I had entered. Though I couldn't feel it was a big mistake, all the same, it *was* a rather dismal showing.

The press coverage was better than what the Beattie circuit usually got, and I must say, the reaction of the spectators was enthusiastic. The fans seemed to understand that it would take me a while to get back to my old form. As for the journalists, well, despite the pleasure of Beattie and the others that we were getting so much attention, I was rather disappointed that the coverage wasn't better. Perhaps it would have been had I announced earlier that I was going to race at Aspen, but of course, until the last minute, I didn't know myself. I had let it out back in October that I was going to try a comeback on the Beattie circuit. It was funny how the press greeted *that* announcement. Serge Lang, the dean of ski writers, who covers the sport for the French sports daily, *l'Equipe,* as well as for a number of other papers, met me in Geneva and was really enthusiastic when I told him my plans. There was good coverage on the story in the Geneva papers, the Zurich and other German-language papers in Switzerland, and papers in Germany, Italy, and Austria. But the French paid little attention to it. As we say, *on ne peut pas être prophète dans son pays* (you can't be a prophet in your own country).

I think I told Lang at the time that I would start racing at Vail. I know that's what I told his son Patrick when I left Geneva for Denver. Beattie made that announcement about Aspen at the Denver airport, but that didn't receive much attention. So maybe more papers would have sent reporters if there had been more advance notice. On the other hand, perhaps it was just as well. Everyone seemed to take great pleasure in reporting that I skied poorly. *"Killy n'a pas fait honneur à sa gloire"* wrote one French paper, literally, "Killy did no honor to his glory"—or, in other words, I had added no luster to my reputation. Another headline read, *"A Aspen, Killy rate sa rentrée chez les pros."* This means, "At Aspen, Killy failed in his return to the pros." Still another read, *"Pour ses débuts professionels, Jean-Claude Killy n'a touché qu'une poignée de dollars."* Translation: "For his professional debut, Killy earned only a fistful of dollars." In effect, I won only $225, but that was the least of my worries.

For the slalom the next day, I changed to Rossignol skis. It wasn't that K2 didn't have a good ski. I felt sure that if I had worked out a contract with them, the potential was there. If Michel went to their factory for three weeks, I'd have had a ski that was right for me. But without a contract, the important thing was to find a ski that would behave the way I needed a ski to behave—and to find it quickly. I was going around looking for a good pair of skis and I asked Malcolm Milne if I could borrow a pair of his. He agreed, and I found these far better for me, though still not exactly what I needed. At any rate, I skied much better on them, and in the slalom qualifying round, I had the second best time. In the opening round I faced Malcolm Milne. In the first run, I beat him by .871 of a second. In the second run, he skied off the course and was disqualified. It was kind of ironic that I should beat Malcolm with his own skis.

In the quarterfinals, I faced Pierre Pouteil-Noble, the young French racer from the B team. That should have been an easy one for me. But I caught a tip on one of the jumps and took a very hard fall. One of the reporters there wrote, "Seeing Killy ski on his head made the day for many of the pros." I don't know if that writer was repeating what any of the other competitors told him, but I imagine there were some who took pleasure in my misfortunes. That didn't bother me. I knew I wasn't skiing well, but all the same, I was beginning to regain my confidence. Maybe the attitude of the other racers actually helped me because many of my skiing problems stemmed from a lack of aggressiveness. I was leaning too much to the inside, had too much upper body motion, and was off in my balance and timing. All of these things were related to my attitude. I used to be called a "psych artist." I was good at making the *other* racers nervous in part because *I* was confident of winning. Well, now my problem was in psyching myself to be confident enough to fight these guys. Unless I had a positive approach, unless I skied aggressively with my weight always poised to move forward or backward as the terrain and the course demanded, I couldn't win. At Aspen, I saw I was better than the others; all I had to do was regain my old form. The result of what the reporters were writing and what the other competitors were saying was that I went to Vail angry, determined to do better.

Part of my problem at Aspen, I think, was that I appeared there as an observer. Then, when I decided to race, my frame of mind was still that of a spectator. I was just another tourist. Technically, though things weren't going just right for me, I don't think I was that far off. My problem was to rediscover the right mental attitude, the racing approach that would make me want to beat everybody else. At Aspen, for the most part I didn't know who these other racers were, and at the outset, I had no particular urge to beat them. This had already begun to change by the time I got to Vail.

After the Aspen race, we went right on to Vail where I stayed with another old friend, Clay Freeman. Ever since I've known him, Clay has been a sales representative for various ski equipment manufacturers. I met him the first time I came to the States back in 1965, when I visited the U.S. ski team training camp at Bend, Oregon. Clay was there working for Head Ski Company. All my life I'll remember our first conversation. He was a former marine—I think he told me he had been a frogman or something like that. I know he's a fantastic athlete, particularly in water sports. Anyway, he said to me, "I'm in love with an Austrian girl, and this summer I'm going back there to pick her up."

"Do you have the money to do that?" I asked.

"I'm a very strong swimmer. And even if I have to swim over to get her, I will," he said. And he wasn't joking. He meant it. His wife, Anneliese—he did get over there and marry her— is a great skier, and ever since then, we have all been good friends. Since Michel and I were still independents, having no sponsors when we arrived at Vail, Clay knew we had to economize, so he very kindly offered us a room in his house.

At Vail, once again I didn't get as much of a chance to practice running gates as I should have. I had to spend some time with Bill Johnson of *Sports Illustrated*—time well spent, I must say, because Bill did a very warm piece on my return to racing. He tried to shoot for getting my picture on the cover, but it didn't work out. Nevertheless, it was very nice coverage in a very important publication. So even though I had to take time away from badly needed training, I couldn't begrudge it.

My equipment was also keeping me off the slopes. I had spoken to Gérard Rubaud about getting me some skis at Vail, and he saw to it that I had them. Having borrowed Malcolm Milne's skis with such success, now I borrowed a pair of his Trappeur boots and Michel tried to fit me by injecting them with polyurethane foam. Next day, we practiced giant slalom on Vail's Golden Peak, where the races were to be held. My first pair of skis—210-cm Roc 550s—were too soft. A second pair were better. But the boots were killing me. Michel worked them over, and still they hurt. The next day, we had free skiing but I couldn't do much because my boots bothered me so. We tried injecting them with a different foam.

But things were improving. On December 2, for the giant slalom, I had the best qualifying time. I went all the way to the finals before losing to Harald Stuefer. The starting system was still troubling me some, and on the second run, after finishing in a virtual tie on the first run, I started out of the gate too soon. My arm hit the barrier, and the strap of my pole twisted up my arm. It took me two gates to get the pole back into my hand and by that time, Stuefer had shot ahead. I still should have beaten him since I was in the faster lane this time. In the Killy Challenge, I had given skiers better than Stuefer an even greater lead and had still beaten them. But in this race, I wasn't skiing properly, and I was tired. I don't think I could have beaten Stuefer that day even if I hadn't had that trouble with my ski pole in the starting gate.

Next day, in the slalom, I got into the semifinals against Spider Sabich. Again I had trouble in the start, only this time it resulted in my crashing into a gatekeeper. Fortunately, no one was hurt, but that put me out of the championship round. In the consolation round, I faced Dan Mooney, one of these young Americans I had never heard of till then. I repeated the run I had against Sabich almost exactly—except that this time, when I fell, the gatekeeper got out of my way. So, for the two days at Vail, I had a second and a fourth worth thirty points and $2,500. Michel was overjoyed. I was pleased at my improvement, but I couldn't understand why Michel was acting as if I had just won.

"I was skiing terribly, Michel. Why are you so pleased?" I asked him.

"Because now I know you can do it," he said. "I know you're not skiing well. We don't have the right equipment yet and we haven't even begun to work at getting you skiing properly again. Agreed. But still, you almost won. When we get your skis, your boots, your timing all straightened out, it won't be close. This proves you're going to win."

And no matter how much I told him I wasn't satisfied with a second, let alone a fourth, I couldn't persuade him; I couldn't tone down his elation. I know now he was right. What mattered was that I had my old drive back—my concentration, my will to win. When Michel saw how much I hated to be second, it only reinforced his conviction that I had passed a critical turning point. He knew I did as well as I did at Vail only because of my attitude. Technically, I was far below my capabilities. But Michel never had any doubts on this score. What he couldn't know beforehand was whether I would get my old fight back. At Aspen, Michel wondered what was on my mind. He was sure I wasn't thinking about the course. At Vail, he saw me make mistakes, but, on the first day at least, he didn't feel these were errors of concentration. He was so elated, he buoyed my spirits up, too. "We're going to win, Jean-Claude," he kept saying. "We're going to win."

On December 4, we took a plane back to France. I had a whole month to work on my technique and find the right skis. At least, I counted on almost a whole month because the next race, at Mt. Snow, was scheduled for January 5. But first off,

I had to go to Val d'Isère for the Critérium de la Première Neige, where I was involved in public relations work: helping to lay out the course, greeting people, forerunning the downhill (a sort of honorary gesture where a former champion runs through the course just before the official race begins), and things of that nature. On top of everything else, I caught a very bad cold and had to go to bed. Meantime, though, Michel and Gérard Rubaud were working on getting me skis. We were pretty happy with the Rossignol Roc 550, a combination metal and fiberglass ski, for giant slalom. But we hadn't liked Rossignol's slalom skis. Now Michel tried out the ST 650 model and the Strato, and decided the Strato worked much better for my style of skiing.

Michel also worked out an arrangement for setting up dual slalom courses with built-in bumps. He had the cooperation of my father's old friend Louis Erny, the head of the sports club at Val d'Isère. Now that we knew what the pro courses were like, we felt it would be best to train on runs that were as nearly like the Beattie courses as we could make them. By December 12, these courses were ready, and Alain Penz and René Techer tried them out. Next day, I ran through the slalom courses six times, for a total of 180 gates, alternating courses with Penz. The following day, I did the same on the giant slalom courses. We had set them up at La Daille, a fairly new area that connects with Bellevarde Mountain halfway between Val d'Isère and Tignes. There was always a large crowd watching us, which I think proves that this format would go over well in Europe, the contrary opinion of many French journalists notwithstanding. For sure, the resort people were very happy to have us there, and they were glad to cooperate by lending us ski patrolmen to set the gates back up and keep the course properly packed. We had a Poma lift that ran the length of the course, too, so we had no wasted time.

I was also working out in the gym, jogging, and doing calisthenics. Having had the experience of running nine courses in a day—almost 300 gates—for two days in a row (that's what I did at Vail), I still had a long way to go to build up my strength and endurance. But the chief task I had was simply to run gates. On December 17, I ran through 450 gates. I did the same thing the next day, when Rubaud came over with a video camera. After lunch and some free skiing, we played back the video to analyze my errors. This was very helpful because Michel and I were finding it a bit difficult to understand one another. We no longer had the same frames of reference when we spoke about snow conditions or the way the skis reacted. There had been considerable technological change in ski design since I had raced, and I wasn't familiar with what they were supposed to do on different snows. And when Michel would try the equipment for me, he was no longer familiar with how I reacted. After all, for over four years now, he had been working with skiers who had very different capabilities from mine. By watching the films together and discussing how the skis were reacting and how I was responding in turn, we began to bridge the technical abyss that had grown between us in these intervening years. For this new equipment—the foam core skis, in particular—did require some adjustment in technique. The newer sidecuts meant your weight had to be somewhat farther back than I was used to skiing. But these were changes we easily made once we could see together what was happening on the snow.

We tried to ski dual slalom all the time. When René Techer caught the grippe, we telephoned Pouteil-Noble to come train with us, since Penz didn't always show up. I found when I trained all alone, I tended to tire more easily. We weren't timing ourselves, so another advantage of having another racer alongside is that we could tell how well we were skiing by comparison to the other guy. Since Penz was one of the best, and since I was having no trouble keeping up with him, I felt pretty good about my chances.

Perhaps I should explain something about slalom racing. A *gate* is not a swinging barrier hung on hinges; it is simply two poles set in the snow, each set of two poles representing one gate. (In *single pole* slalom, your skis pass on alternate sides of a series of single poles instead of through a gate.) Each pair of poles is topped by flags of the same color, or the poles can be colored. The skis must always pass between the two poles of each gate; it is the skier's option which way he wants to enter the gate, though in any course, there will be only one way that is the fastest. It is permissable to knock down a pole as long as your skis pass between the two poles of a gate. If both skis don't pass between the two poles, if you straddle one pole for instance, you have missed the gate. If the gatekeeper sees it, you are disqualified. An *open gate* is one where a line drawn between the two poles of the gate would be at a right angle to the fall line (the line a ball would take freely rolling down the hill). A *closed gate* would be one where the line between the two poles of the gate would be more or less in the direction of the fall line. A series of closed gates is called a *flush*. In slalom, the gates are set close together, requiring almost constant turning all the way down the course. In downhill, there are very few gates, and the ones that are there are mainly to control the direction of the racer and to slow him down where it would be dangerous to go all out. In downhill, the top speeds are sometimes in excess of eighty miles an hour. In slalom, because of the constant turning, speeds rarely exceed thirty miles an hour. Giant slalom is a discipline halfway between the two: gates are set at greater intervals than in slalom, but giant slalom is still a test of efficient turning. Giant slalom speeds rarely exceed fifty miles an hour. In professional racing, there is less difference between the slalom and giant slalom courses than in amateur racing. The courses are shorter than in FIS competition and generally not as steep; therefore, the speeds are not as great. An FIS slalom drops about 600 vertical feet and has between sixty and seventy gates; a GS drops about 1,350 vertical feet with about forty-five gates. Most of Beattie's slaloms had a little over thirty gates; most of his giant slaloms had a little under thirty gates.

On December 20, I ran through 608 slalom gates—sixteen runs of thirty-eight gates each. That was more gates than I had ever skied in one day in my life. And it included going over forty-eight jumps. Michel was ecstatic. "Jean-Claude," he told me, "you're anticipating your turns now. You're in balance all the time. You're skiing like the Killy of 1967."

Michel had been worried about my balance and wanted me to do more free skiing, but there just wasn't time. His comment about my anticipating my turns was technical talk about getting my upper body moving in the direction of each turn so that I could edge and weight my skis properly, bending them into the precise curve of the turn I was about to make. I could tell Michel was worried we weren't doing enough work, and when I heard these remarks after our session of the 20th, I was greatly relieved.

The next day, all I had strength for was a couple of hours of work in the morning—a total of 270 gates of giant slalom. I was skiing well, but it was evident I didn't have the stamina to put together another day like the day before. I was turning more automatically now, and my giant slalom skis—the 210-cm Roc 550s—seemed to be just right. Michel left to go back to his home in Thonon to celebrate Christmas with his family, but I continued to run gates. I rested the day before Christmas and on Christmas, then continued training right up through the 29th. I tried Jean Noël Augert's skis (Augert was the reigning slalom ace on the French team) on the last day and liked them very much. I told Rossignol I wanted them to make a pair for me with the same characteristics.

I had pretty much decided to go with Rossignol after the Vail race, but we negotiated back and forth for a while because I wasn't completely satisfied with the skis I had tried—or with the money they had offered me. Nevertheless, it looked as though they had the best capability of making the kind of skis Michel and I felt we needed, and I ended up signing with them. They knew I was pretty desperate by that time, which helps explain why they didn't offer me much. It was probably the worst contract I'd ever signed. I was getting no more for my equipment contracts as a pro than I had received as an amateur. This was inequitable from two points of view. First, as I've noted, today's amateurs are making more—from what I hear, some of today's racers get in the neighborhood of $100,000. Second, a company can do much more from an advertising point of view with an openly professional skier than with an amateur who still has to abide by some rules, hypocritical though they may be. It is still against the rules to mention a skier's name or use his picture in an ad for the product. Gustavo Thoeni, for example, won the World Cup for three years in a row. He skis on Spalding skis. But Spalding can't show his picture or advertise that Thoeni won the World Cup on Spalding skis. Instead, they say, "Spalding is still Numero Uno." They pretend that the ski, not the racer, won the World Cup. But if I would win a race, Rossignol could advertise, "At Mt. Snow, Jean-Claude Killy was first in the giant slalom on Rossignol skis." And they could show race pictures with both my face and the Rossignol label clearly identifiable. I'm convinced that in the long run, equipment manufacturer money has got to go to the professionals. I also believe that in the long run, this will help make amateur racing truly amateur. Maybe that's why some ski federation people, such as Jean Vuarnet, are so opposed to professional racing. They fear it will dry up sources of money for their operation.

Both professional racing and Jean-Claude Killy must have been question marks to Rossignol at the beginning of the 1973 season, so I suppose they can't be blamed for driving a hard bargain. The contract figure apart, our relations were very good for the rest of the season. The most important thing was that they did everything in their power to cooperate with Michel, to see to it that I had the skis I needed.

On December 30, I returned to my home in Geneva and prepared for my return to the States. René Techer came over on the 31st, and that night we opened three or four bottles of champagne to celebrate the new year.

"Here's to the new pro champion," Danièle toasted. I drank to that, and the next day I left for Boston.

6
LOST: THE WINNING TOUCH

WITH my win in the giant slalom at Mt. Snow, I felt I was on my way. I didn't expect things to be easy, but I knew then that I could put it all together and ski consistently well for the nine runs necessary for a first place. I had the technique and the strength. Proof came the next day in the slalom when I again had the best qualifying time. I saw myself rolling up a string of victories. What had seemed almost unattainable a month before now seemed so easy.

In the opening round I faced Spider Sabich, who had had a poor qualifying time and was skiing badly. Spider, the reigning pro champion, was going to be Spider the ex-champion, I thought. As I faced him in the starting gate, I said to myself, "We won't be hearing any more from you." I was full of confidence, I must admit. So much so, on the first run, I wasn't concentrating properly and had difficulty in one of the gates on the upper part of the course.

What a shock! Spider beat me by almost a full second. I came out of my reverie and realized I was going to have to ski for my victories. For the second run, I bore down with all I had. One of the writers later reported this was probably the best run anyone had all day. I felt sure I had overcome Spider's lead to beat him in the combined time for the two runs.

But that wasn't the case. Spider had won by .024 of a second. What had happened was curious—sort of the reverse of the situation I had with Pepi Steigler on the Killy Challenge. As al-

The first professional race:
Aspen, Colorado.

The many moods of Jean-Claude Killy: ISRA at Vail, Colorado, December 197

A tense moment at the Steamboat Springs, Colorado, race.

The award stand, Steamboat Springs, Colorado. Left to right: Dan Mooney, Jean-Claude Killy, Tyler Palmer.

Good friend Jean-Pierre with Killy, Steamboat Springs, Colorado.

Michel Arpin, Killy's tutor and friend, makes a point.

Running gates at Breckenridge, Colorado, winter of 1972, before the comebac

Killy at Breckenridge, Colorado.

At the Aspen, Colorado, race.

Ian Todd.

The Rossignol team.

Killy and Danièle in a festive mood.

Danièle Gaubert, the future Mme Killy.

Downhill with turns.
(Copyright by Willis A. Wood.)

Part of a racer's life: Waiting.
(Copyright by Willis A. Wood.)

Gold medal winner and friend Stein Eriksen jokes with Killy.

Killy with Ethel Kennedy.

With his father, Robert Killy.

Killy with his old rival, Karl Schranz.

Racing through the fog at the first Aspen, Colorado, race.

ways, I had checked the finish line to see where the electric eye beam was, and it seemed to me it was high. But Beattie was using very sophisticated timing devices and Spider was thoroughly familiar with them. They would register when anything from the ski up to the head passed the finish line. Knowing this, Spider turned his skis up on edge as he neared the finish so that the device would register the time the moment his ski tips crossed the line. For me, it registered when my body went through. The difference between our two combined times represented about a foot; thus, Spider won because of his experience.

Of course, if I had been concentrating as I should have in the first run, it wouldn't have mattered. I would have been far enough ahead not to have been beaten by my ignorance about the timing mechanism. But it was a good lesson for me. I wasn't going to let that happen again.

Later, I was told that shortly after I lost to Spider, a little boy, not more than four years old, went up to the ISRA announcer and asked him if I had run yet. It was still very cold out and the poor little fellow must have been half frozen. When the announcer told him, "Sorry, son, Killy is through for the day," his face just fell as though he'd lost his pet dog.

Well, when I heard that story, I was terribly disappointed, too. Not just that I would have liked to have won two in a row, to have won the extra points and the extra money. Sure, that's what I was racing for. But I also like to win for the people who are rooting for me, particularly the little kids who come to see me race. When I can give them pleasure, it gives me the feeling that I'm giving something back to the sport in return for what the sport had given me. And so, for that boy's sake, I was particularly sorry my lack of concentration, overconfidence, tiredness from the preceding day—whatever it was—had caused me to make that error in my first run against Spider.

There were to be a couple of weeks off between Mt. Snow and the next race, scheduled for January 21 at Hunter Mountain in New York State's Catskill Mountains. Michel went back to France to see what he could do about getting me better skis from Rossignol. Meantime, Danièle joined me. This was according to the schedule we had agreed on, but I was pleased I had taken a first before her arrival. It put me in a better mood and made me easier to live with.

Of course, Danièle was very happy over my Mt. Snow result. She knew how hard I had worked for it, and knowing how much it meant to me, it made her happy, too. But to tell the truth, I think Danièle just assumed all along that I was going to win. She never had a moment's doubt—she was just sure that whatever I had to do to get back into winning form, I would do—and I would succeed. Michel's confidence in me was the astute estimate of a man who knew exactly what it would take: how much work on equipment, on technique, on conditioning. Danièle's confidence was more like blind faith. All the same, having her around again was very good for my morale. As it turned out, I was going to need all the support I could get.

In the overall standings, on leaving Mt. Snow, Stuefer was in first place (he had gone on to beat Sabich in the slalom final) with ninety points and $8,175 in winnings. I was second with seventy-two points and $5,950, and Sabich was third, five points behind me. Despite my slow start, I wasn't all that far behind. Though I hadn't announced it yet, I was gunning for the Grand Prix, and coming out of Mt. Snow, I was sure it was within my grasp.

Before heading for Hunter, I went down to Boone, North Carolina, for a promotion sponsored by the First Union National Bank of North Carolina. It was the second time I had been to Boone to fulfill a contract set up by IMC's representative there, Jack Lester. Lester was quite a promoter, and he made much of the fact that he had arranged an exclusive visit of Jean-Claude Killy to the Carolina hills.

My assignment there was to run through a slalom course —at nearby Appalachian Mountain in the morning and at Sugar Mountain in the afternoon—and set a standard time. Then the ten Southern skiers whose times were nearest mine would get prizes. From the accents of some of these Southerners, they must have been from southern Switzerland, southern Austria, and southern Germany. But none came very close to my time.

I also had to appear at various parties as well as give a ski clinic to the instructors of the French–Swiss Ski College, the rather grandiose name of the ski school that Jack Lester ran at Appalachian Ski Mountain. It was all very pleasant—except for some questions that were raised about how exclusive my appearance was.

As it happened, the pros were scheduled to appear at another nearby ski area, Beach Mountain, in February. Since Lester had said my appearance was exclusive, he tried to scotch the rumors that I would be coming back with the pros by announcing that I had "no further commitments in the area." I suppose that was true, strictly speaking, but the implication that I would not be back for the pro races was not true.

No such ambiguity marred my next appearance, which was in Toronto. Benson & Hedges, the sponsors of the ISRA tour, asked me to go up there for a TV interview designed to drum up interest in the forthcoming race at Collingwood—the one that would follow the Hunter Mountain race. Afterward, Danièle and I ate in a very nice restaurant, and then headed back to the States to a place called Scandinavian Village in Phonecia, New York, about a thirty-minute drive from Hunter. It was a very pleasant motel-ski shop-ski touring complex run by Harry Vallin, the owner of the Scandinavian Ski Shop in New York City. There was a fair restaurant there, and even a nightclub. However, between my sore throat, which was bothering me again, and having to train and race at Hunter, I didn't enjoy it very much.

Hunter was not new to me. I had been there the previous year for an outing organized by *Ladies' Home Journal*. So I knew what to expect. Some of the other Europeans, though, just couldn't believe it. There's this tremendous base lodge with a cafeteria that can feed hundreds. It's an enormous building with a massive stone fireplace. We just don't see that kind of day lodge in Europe. What amazed our guys even more were the snowmaking facilities. There had been a thaw in the East (it happens just about every year, I understand—so regularly, it's called the "January thaw"), and there wasn't much snow left. But the Hunter snowmaking plant is so big that it can cover the mountain overnight.

The thaw gave us some problems during practice. Michel had come back from France with a slew of new skis for me to try. But the snow was so wet, we couldn't really tell how the skis were reacting. Nevertheless, Michel thought I was riding my skis better than I had at Mt. Snow where, he felt despite good results, I was still leaning too much to the inside of my turns. His observations surprised me because I wasn't comfortable skiing on this wet man-made snow which seemed to scoot out from under my skis. Nobody, for that matter, seemed to be skiing well.

The day of the giant slalom, it turn colder and began to snow. That wasn't so good for my sore throat, but it was much better for my skiing. I don't know if it was from the aspirin I was taking for my cold or from the antibiotics I was taking for my throat or just a reflection of my run-down feeling, but my reflexes seemed to be late. At any rate, in the semifinals, I lost to Perry Thompson.

In the consolation round for third place, I faced Spider Sabich again. Going into this race, Spider was only five points behind me in the overall standings, so it was rather important that I beat him. Besides, I was still smarting from our last meeting in the slalom at Mt. Snow. I wanted this victory very much.

I stayed as close to the poles as I could to gain every inch. So close, in fact, that near the top of the course, my knee knocked one of the poles down (this is perfectly legal as long as my two skis pass between the two poles of the gate). I had a good run—good enough to win, I thought. But the gatekeeper at the top of the course ruled that I had straddled the pole I knocked down with my knee. There were four or five other racers standing by the sidelines at the time—Tyler Palmer, I know, was one of them—and they told me there was no question I was right.

I appealed to the jury. I told them this gatekeeper was inexperienced, that certainly after all my years of racing I would know the difference between straddling a gate and legally knocking down a pole. But the gatekeeper stuck to his story and the officials upheld him. With that kind of officiating, I wasn't going to run away with the pro title for sure. Nor was this to be the last time that poor judging affected the results. The fault was not Hunter Mountain's; they did a good job of preparing the courses. But a truly professional league shouldn't expect to pick up competent race officials at each stop along the circuit. In my opinion, the course officials should be a permanent part of the ISRA staff, experienced in the format of the pro races, and traveling with the racers from one area to the next along with the announcers, PR people, and so forth.

This unfair ruling would have been more serious had I been in contention for first place. As it was, this improper disqualification simply meant that Spider and I were now tied for second overall, both of us having gained on Stuefer, who lost in the quarterfinals. The championship round was fought between the two rookie Americans, Dan Mooney and Perry Thompson. Mooney, skiing extremely well, took the victory.

It was no fluke for Mooney; he beat Tschudi, Penz, and Sabich to get into the finals. Though he had never been any more than a B team hopeful as an amateur, here he was beating world champions like Penz and myself and seasoned pros like Sabich. This had to be good for pro racing for it was bound to attract other up and coming young skiers. The next best thing to winning myself was to see rookies like Mooney and Thompson doing so well.

For the slalom the next day, the course had iced over. Though it was cold, it was also sunny, and there was a big crowd. Going into the race, I felt much stronger. My throat was still sore, but my sinuses had cleared somewhat and I no longer felt like an invalid, as though I should properly have stayed in bed.

I faced Mooney in the quarterfinals and was immediately put to the test, for he was still skiing very solidly. In the first run, he beat me by .15 of a second. In the second run, he got ahead of me again, and I remember thinking that he was going to be more dangerous than I had expected. But the pressure on him must have been too much: he was pushing so hard, he spun out of one gate, allowing me to pass him and win easily.

In the semifinals, I raced against Otto Tschudi. I got a good rhythm going and beat him in the first run by .650 of a second. I was ahead again on the second run when I caught a tip and twisted out of my ski. Some journalists reported that I fell because my binding popped open. It was the other way around, and it was a good thing that the binding released. As it was, I hurt my ankle, and when I faced Kurt Recher, an Austrian who skis for Hunter Mountain and was, therefore, a local favorite, I made the same error, catching a tip on the gate at the first jump. It spun me around and out of the race into fourth place.

It was funny, but during the course of the season, I frequently found myself making the same mistake twice in a row. Or if Michel made a point of warning me about a particular spot on the course, that's where I would get into trouble. Where I would ski best, no matter how difficult the course, was where I had convinced myself beforehand that I would *not* have any difficulties. For me, a positive approach seemed to be essential to victory. Any doubts, and that's where I'd get hung up.

Tshudi beat out Thompson for first place. Both Sabich and Stuefer had been eliminated in the first round. So I left Hunter still in second place, but now only ten points behind Stuefer, and once again five points ahead of Sabich.

From Hunter, we drove to Toronto, a long drive that took us all day. We stayed in a very interesting motel that night. We were dead tired and decided to have our meal in the room, and we were surprised to find not only that the food was good, but there was an excellent wine list. Sharing a Cadet Mouton Rothschild, we really relaxed after the tiring day. When we went to turn on the TV, we discovered it would play tapes, and there was a choice of films we could watch. You simply called down to the desk and they would set up the program for you and put it on your bill. It was the first time I had seen this kind of set in a motel, and it made for a very pleasant evening.

The contrast couldn't have been more striking when we discovered our accommodations the next day after driving to Collingwood. The Rossignol people in Canada had made the arrangements, and they were ridiculous. We had a brand new house—it really wasn't completed yet. We had to wade through mud up to our knees to get in the front door, and inside it was worse! Just bare walls and some beds—no other furniture, no chairs, no bed lamps, nothing. So we spent the next day looking for a better place to stay. We finally found a fairly decent motel, but that first night was pretty uncomfortable.

Blue Mountain, the ski area where the race was to be held, was another surprise. In Canada at the end of January, I expected it to be bitter cold with snow covering everything. Instead it was warm, and the only snow we saw was a little patch in the middle of one of the slopes. When we got there, an instructor was out there with one of his students. There was barely room for him to make two turns. Just this little circle of white with brown grass and rocks and bare trees everywhere else. There wasn't even enough snow to train on. We didn't even realize Collingwood could make snow because none of the snowmaking equipment was in evidence. It turned out, this was because it was too warm and they were waiting for the temperature to drop, but initially it was very disconcerting.

Our accommodations were bad, the slope conditions were bad, and my health was still bad. I began to empathize with the American ski team members who go over to Europe on the World Cup circuit and have to live out of their suitcases or backpacks, always eating strange food, having to talk a foreign tongue, never settling in one place long enough to feel at home. This trip was beginning to feel that way to me. I couldn't shake my cold and sore throat. I'm sure that at least one reason for that was the inability to follow my normal diet, to keep my normal habits, to sleep and relax in my normal way.

The night before the race, it finally turned cold enough to make snow, and for the giant slalom the course wasn't too bad. The day of the race was foggy and chilly, but there still must have been close to 10,000 people there—the largest attendance of the season. And I'm afraid those who came to watch me were disappointed. I made the qualifying round and that was about all. I faced Malcolm Milne in the opening round. Malcolm, like most of the other racers, had had difficulty in the qualifying round because of a very steep section right at the start. It hadn't bothered me, though, and my qualifying time had been very good. But when I raced against Malcolm, I skied terribly and he skied very well. And that was the end of the race for me.

It was very discouraging. Michel began to wonder if all our

work was going down the drain. The only consolation I had that day was that Spider Sabich was beaten for first by Pierre Pouteil-Noble.

This phenomenon seems to have baffled a lot of people. How could unknowns like Pouteil-Noble or Mooney or Thompson beat guys like me or Sabich? For some journalists, this was supposed to be the proof that we were over the hill. Yet the young generation of really first rate amateurs like Penz or Billy Kidd before him or Tyler Palmer or Hank Kashiwa—these guys were turning out to be quite mediocre on the pro circuit. How come?

I think the answer is simple: although both have snow, skiers, and gates, pro and amateur are totally different skiing sports. The pro racer has to have super-fast reflexes to get out of that starting gate fast. In amateur racing, you have to get a good start, too, but it doesn't matter whether or not you start instantaneously when you hear the "go" signal. The clock doesn't start running until you break the beam. An amateur can delay his start and still be fast out of the gate. Or he can start instantly and be slow leaving the gate. In pro racing, the clock starts from the time the gate opens, whether or not you go through it. Some very good amateur racers never did adjust to this difference.

And then there's the element of the guy on the next course. Since you don't want to take any unnecessary risks, you've got to assess your opponent accurately. It becomes a psychological game as well as a skiing contest. And finally, there's this factor of consistency. Being able to stand up run after run—under pressure. These were the main differences, not the courses, which rarely presented any serious technical problem other than their flatness, the jumps, and occasionally bad snow preparation. There was just no predicting how a guy would ski in the pros by looking at his amateur record. World Cup ski racing and dual slalom pro racing were two totally different sports.

For the slalom the next day, it was more like Canadian weather. It had turned much colder. First the course iced up and then it snowed, resulting in a very unpredictable surface. Again it was very steep at the top, and a lot of skiers came to grief. But once again, I had a very good qualifying time, the best on my course, and I faced Egon Zimmermann in the opening round. When I was first making a name in the amateurs, Egon was already a star. In 1958, at Zurs, I remember following him down the mountain. At that time, his was the number one name in skiing. But now, he was well into his thirties and not likely to be a threat. And, in effect, he fell and was disqualified, moving me into the quarterfinals against Hugo Nindl.

Nindl was a hot and cold skier, and this was one of his hot days. But he could have been skiing poorly and it wouldn't have mattered because on the second run, I caught a tip at the very top part of the course—the tricky steep section that had caused so many to disqualify the day before. And that was it for me at Collingwood.

Disastrous. My script called for me to get better and better after Mt. Snow, and instead, I was skiing miserably. When I caught that tip, I was using a skating technique to gain speed coming out of the starting gate. I always used to do this as an amateur, but there the courses are set so there is more room between the starting gate and the first gate on the course.

In the finals, Sabich beat out Stuefer to take the lead in the overall standing with 132 points. Stuefer was close behind with 129 points. I was now in third place with 104 points. The old pros that I had counted out were still very much alive and kicking. And I was thoroughly disgusted with myself. I was making one little mistake after another. I had my determination back, and for the most part, my concentration. But there would be lapses. I had become careless; I forgot how racing demanded complete absorption. I forgot that you had to be precise in every move you made from the starting gate to the bottom, that you had to think every inch of the way, concentrating totally on every gate.

Collingwood made me remember.

7
GETTING IT BACK

I WAS disappointed that I hadn't done better at Collingwood, but one thing I know from years of racing—you never rerun a lost race. You had a bad weekend? Tough. But there's another weekend coming. And that's what I had to start thinking about.

Of course, Michel and I would spend some time right after a race analyzing what went wrong. I don't mean that I try to pretend it didn't happen. But once we were satisfied that we understood what was at fault—and in this case, it was just a lack of concentration, of consistency in my skiing—then it was pack up and on to the next race.

And that next race was quite a surprise. The race was at Buck Hill, just outside of St. Paul. Nothing I had seen in the ski world had prepared me for Buck Hill. We almost didn't see it! In fact, Peter Duncan, one of the Canadian racers, drove twenty miles past the area before a policeman directed him back.

Buck Hill was not what you could call a mountain. From top to bottom, it was only 310 feet—less than 100 meters. In the Alps, every ski area of any importance has at least ten times as much *dénivelation*—the distance from top to bottom, or what American skiers call the vertical drop. At Tignes, near my home in France, the vertical is over twenty times as great. At Buck Hill, you drive on an interstate highway—a *flat* interstate, I should point out—practically into the area's parking lot! We stayed in a Holiday Inn, lived right in the middle of a big city, got on a highway, and drove right into the area. I had never imagined entering a ski race in that kind of setting.

To me, everything new is exciting, and I was fascinated there could be skiing at such a place. Besides, our stay in St. Paul was pleasant in every way. Tom Krebsbach, a Chevrolet dealer whom I had met during my work for General Motors, came out to meet us at the airport with cars to pick us up and get us around town. Tom and I had become very good friends—he visits me in Europe every year—and he went out of his way in every respect to make things enjoyable. He not only took us to our motel and the area, but arranged for us to work out in a local gym where we played handball and tennis, did some running, and had a sauna. In the evening, he showed us around town, and one night he threw a party for us. It made a difference in my morale.

Despite the smallness of the area, the course at Buck Hill turned out to be a real challenge, though at first, none of us realized it. The course at Mt. Snow had seemed flat, but this was an ice hockey rink by comparison. It was short—only 19 gates for the giant slalom—and there were no steep pitches at all. I've already discussed one problem posed by a flat course, that of keeping your speed up all the time. If you make a single mistake, you lose speed and there's no way you can get it back.

Contradictory though it may sound, a flat course poses another problem. A skier without the technique to ski a more demanding course might manage to luck through something like this one at Buck Hill. Since it was so short, it was possible that a lesser skier could make it through with a good time. Disqualifications were unlikely. Proof is that ten of the sixteen races were so close, they had to be decided on the basis of combined times.

So far on the pro tour, we had not come across a single course where waxing the skis was very important to the outcome. But here at Buck Hill, Michel was convinced getting the right wax would be critical. The bottom of a ski has a plastic material—polyethylene—which normally slides fairly well on snow. But it can be made much more slippery by applying a wax. Which wax is the most slippery depends on the temperature and quality of the snow and air. In a long downhill race, guessing the right wax can be the difference between victory and defeat. On a short slalom, it usually doesn't matter very much. On this flat course, though, because the racers' times would be very close to one another, Michel was sure wax would spell the difference, and Michel is tops at figuring out which is the right wax to use.

A lot of the racers hated this course. Alain Penz, for example, couldn't qualify. He just wasn't versatile enough for this kind of racing. He was used to putting his skis on edge. But if your skis had too much bite on this course, you were through. Hugo Nindl, who has a reputation for skiing well on flat sections, was asked after the race if he still preferred flat courses to steep ones. "Yeah, I like them flat," he said, "but not this flat."

The race was sponsored by some McDonald's hamburger dealers in the St. Paul area. They must have had some special influence somewhere because the weather, which we had expected to be frigid and bleak, was just perfect—clear skies, mild, no wind. I was disappointed in the turnout. The McDonald dealers had put up about $40,000 in prize money and advertising, but only about 3,200 spectators showed up on Saturday. I heard that the hamburger dealers were pleased, but most of the racers felt that an area as accessible as Buck Hill should have produced a crowd of more than twice that many people.

In the qualifying round, I skied fantastically. On a course that took only twenty-two seconds, I had a margin on the field of .7 of a second. Word got around that I was really fast today. Yet, in the opening round against Dan Mooney, I was surprised to find many in the crowd were cheering for Mooney instead of for me. This was doubly curious. First, this Minnesota crowd seemed strangely quiet most of the time. Second, Mooney, after all, is not very well known and up to this point hadn't had any noticeable following among the spectators. In fact, I was generally the favorite, in part because I was the best known, but also, I think, because the public thought it was very sporting of me to give these young racers a chance to beat me. Yet here, the crowd was rooting for my opponent, an unknown. I wondered whether the Minneapolis–St. Paul region had been settled by Austrians or had any other reason to be anti-French. Later on, the mystery was explained when I learned Mooney was born in Minneapolis; a lot of his friends had come out to root for him. Another local, Spencer Butts, faced Harald Stuefer in the opening and also drew a lot of cheers.

The cheers weren't much help, though. Both Stuefer and I won in the opening round. I went on to beat Ken Corrock, former U.S. team member whose sister Susan won a bronze medal in downhill in the Sapporo Olympics; Malcolm Milne, who had beaten Stuefer in the quarterfinals; and in the championship round, the old flat-course master himself, Hugo Nindl. It was a very demanding day—technically as well as physically. On this very modest hill, there had been some great racing, and of course a great result for me. After the disaster at Collingwood, this restored my morale.

After the local favorites, Mooney and Butts, had been eliminated, I was gratified to see the crowd was again with me. Just before the championship round, one of the spectators even broke through the cordon around the starting area to seek me out for an autograph. Michel was there to intercept him and really cussed him out—in French, fortunately, so no one understood what he was saying. I get approached more than all the other racers combined in this respect, and except when I'm actually on the course (as in this case), I always try to be pleasant. When I sign my autograph, I thank people for having asked me for it. Sometimes, I'll pose for pictures with people if they ask. Some of the journalists have asked me why I do this. They're amazed that I don't just act the prima donna and insist on my privacy.

Frankly, I often wish people would respect my privacy more. But when they don't, I'm amazed that anyone should question why I behave the way I do. The public pays to see me. My contracts are what they are because of my popularity. I suspect if I were rude, the public wouldn't be so anxious to see me, and my value to my financial backers would drop. I don't mean to sound calculating or crass. I don't think of these things every time I sign an autograph or answer some fan's question. I'm naturally polite and I'd probably act this way even if it weren't directly in my interest to do so.

The point is, it *is* in my interest, so why should the press constantly comment about how amazing it is that I have so much patience with the public? To me, that's just part of being a good professional. Some industry people tell me that they think I'm much more gracious with the public now than I used to be. They say it's a sign I have matured. Perhaps they're right, though I don't consciously act any differently now from the way I always did. I suspect that in the period immediately after my Olympic victories, when demands on my time—and on my privacy—were heaviest, fatigue was frequently interpreted as disdain. In truth, my attitude on this question has always been the same.

What can be said, though, is that public attention meant I had far fewer opportunities to relax than the other competitors. I was more in demand for interviews from the press as well as for autographs for the fans. And at times, that took its toll.

For the slalom on Sunday, it was another nice day. This time, the crowd was bigger—perhaps 5,000 people. And for the first time, we had live television; WTCN-TV, the local Metromedia outlet, was covering the event. It looked like there would be lots of drama when Sabich had the best qualifying time on this course and I again had the best on mine.

In the opening round, Sabich faced Tyler Palmer and beat him. I faced Mickey Schwaiger and took the first run fairly easily. But in the second run, a curious thing happened. Because I had beaten Schwaiger going away in the first run, I thought the lower part of his course must be slower. This slalom was set directly in the fall line. It was only 250 yards long, and with twenty-two gates. This made it very tight, with the last jump leading into a very tight final section.

When we switched courses for the second run and I saw that Schwaiger was running about even with me in the upper part of the course, I therefore figured the only way to win, considering that the last part of the course was slower on my side, was to take some risks, stay very close to the gates, and really push coming off the last jump. Unfortunately, I caught a tip right near the end, flipped into the air, knocked down a gatekeeper, and plowed into the crowd.

Later, Michel told me I was wrong about the speed of the two courses. The one I was on was actually faster at the bottom. A very foolish miscalculation. My real error, though, was in not ignoring the other guy and just running my own race.

Spider went on to win and take the lead from Stuefer. I remained in third place.

It was at Buck Hill that I announced I had signed with Rossignol. I was asked if this meant I was a member of Team Rossignol, the official name of the group Rubaud had put together with sponsorship by Trappeur boots, Look Nevada bindings, and Mossant clothes. On my own I had signed with Trappeur and Rossignol. I had always used Look Nevada bindings and still had a contract with them even before I went on the pro circuit.

But I also had a valid and continuing contract with Mighty Mac ski clothes, so I could not be an official member of Team Rossignol even though I now traveled with them, trained with them, and in every other way acted like a full-fledged member of the team. My points were included in the Team Rossignol points, too, so when I was asked what it meant to be sponsored by Rossignol, Trappeur, and Look, but not to be an official member of Team Rossignol, I answered, "I'm part of the team and my heart is with the team, you know, but not my clothing."

The fact is, none of us was very clear about just what the factory team concept meant. Though all the products grouped together were French, Rossignol, which has a worldwide market, didn't want the team to be made up of French skiers only. Thus, the members included Malcolm Milne, an Australian; Dan Mooney, an American; Otto Tschudi, an American-educated Norwegian; as well as Alain Penz, Pierre Pouteil-Noble, and me from France.

The factory teams were in a competition separate from the individual competition. Each factory team's top three finishers in each event would count for point calculations. At the end of the season, a manufacturer's award was to go to the team with the highest points. This was supposed to stimulate more interest, but Rossignol got so far ahead of everybody else so early in the season that it was almost embarrassing.

Most of the factory teams let their skiers make whatever deals they wanted to with other equipment manufacturers. Thus, a racer could represent Hart skis, Allsop bindings, Hanson boots —or whatever other combination he could arrange—and each of these would compute his points for the team standings. Only Rossignol worked out the package deal—except in my case, as I've indicated, all Rossignol skiers had the same group of sponsors.

Though this worked out fine in the race for team points, it posed some other problems. Since all these products were French, most of the nonracers traveling with Team Rossignol were also French. And this led to a certain amount of friction. For example, even though I knew Malcolm for a long time and felt closer to him in many ways than to Penz, there were things that I could take for granted with Penz, just because he was a Frenchman, that I couldn't with Malcolm.

Language had something to do with it, I'm sure. Malcolm got along better with the Americans than he did with the French. But it's more than language. A whole upbringing is involved. Food that Dan Mooney would find perfectly palatable, Penz, Pouteil-Noble, and I would not like—just because we were French. A lot of people say we French are highly individualistic, which I think is true in part, but here we seemed to think alike on many, many things. Gallic traits or otherwise, our personalities and our ways seemed hard for others to accept. There was certainly no esprit in the Team Rossignol that was anything like the group spirit I remember from my French Ski Team days.

Another difference, of course, is that this was a strictly commercial venture. On a national ski team, you feel you're representing your country. Patriotism is a very enobling emotion; you do try harder for love of country. When you're representing a product, you don't feel prouder of your accomplishment for the sake of the company; it just means your negotiating position may be that much stronger.

To tell the truth, I don't really think the team concept has much meaning in skiing even at the amateur level. Alpine skiing is not a team sport; it is an individual sport. The team is simply a vehicle that permits the individual to compete. In amateur racing, the team centralizes the efforts to raise money for the competitors and to provide training places and coaching assistance. It also centralizes the organization of the races, the record-keeping, and other things necessary for the sport to exist. It really wouldn't be possible to have amateur ski racing as we know it without having national teams involved.

But it should be understood that such a team is simply a collection of individual competitors who race against each other as much as against the racers of other teams. The value of team spirit—and it does have a value—is largely psychological. The racer who feels he represents his country as well as himself gains confidence from knowing other good racers also represent his country. Thus, the pressure on him is lessened.

In professional racing, the individual has no direct interest in seeing the team do well. It could be organized that way—by having a monetary prize to the winning team shared by the team members. This would work better if a guy couldn't ski for more than one team, as he can now. The way it is at present, the factory team is merely a convenience for working out contracts, organizing training, and arranging for travel and housing. Naturally, when you live with a bunch of guys over a period of months, you hope they do well in competition with skiers from other teams, but I think a team should be more than this. There is room for a good deal of improvement before this concept takes on any real significance as a force in professional ski racing.

I was still suffering from a sore throat the entire time I was in St. Paul, so Tom Krebsbach arranged for me to go to the hospital for a checkup. He made an appointment for me with a friend of his, Dr. Jack Fee. When I heard the name, I thought how appropriate it was for a doctor, though in this case, out of friendship for Tom and as a gesture of hospitality, there was no fee.

I had quite an enlightening talk with Dr. Fee about my state of health. He gave me some penicillin shots for my infected throat, but he suggested that my real problem was diet. Eating the processed foods one gets in most American restaurants, he said, deprives the body of much of the nourishment it needs. He thought this might be particularly difficult for Europeans who don't have the same eating habits as Americans, who don't drink as much milk, for example, or who might not like the flavor of American cooking and therefore wouldn't eat enough of the things that would provide the necessary nutrition.

It's funny, I had always thought that the French diet was terrible from a health point of view. Our breakfasts—croissants and jelly with *café au lait* (half coffee, half milk with much of the nutrition boiled out of it)—are insubstantial. Our lunches are too heavy, with too many sauces on everything. And we eat too many sweets and drink too much wine.

But at least our vegetables are fresh and our breads aren't baked of super-refined flour. We get lots of protein from fish, cheeses, and other meats besides the ever-present hamburger, and our portions are moderate. When I told Dr. Fee that I thought the hearty American breakfast of fruits and cereals was better than the French custom, he agreed that a good breakfast was important but warned me against many of the packaged cereals.

"They're loaded with sugar so the kids will like them," he pointed out. "But many of them are almost worthless from a nutritional point of view."

I knew that food had been a problem for me on this tour, but I had thought it was mainly a matter of my tastes not being the same as American tastes. Now I knew the problem was more serious.

The next race was to be at Beach Mountain, North Carolina. I thought perhaps the sunshine and warmer weather I might find down there would also help me shake my throat infection, so it was with a good deal of anticipation that I flew from St. Paul to Charlotte. Besides, I knew that Jack Lester would have a fit welcome for us and would see to it that we were comfortable.

True to expectations, Jack was at the airport with a bunch

of Ford Broncos that he had gotten the local Ford dealers to donate for our use. He covered himself on my second "exclusive" appearance by concocting a story about telephoning the French president and arranging for him to send Team Rossignol to Charlotte to race at Beach Mountain.

Now, as a matter of fact, Jack had telephoned President Pompidou—though, of course, he didn't get to talk to him. And, of course, the Rossignol team members, like the rest of the pro racers, were here because it was another stop on the Benson & Hedges tour. I don't know whether any of the newspapermen believed all of Jack's stories, but there were reporters at the airport to greet us, and they had printed the tale about Jack's call to Pompidou.

I hoped the reporters had an easier time understanding us than we had understanding them. There was a little cocktail party and hors d'oeuvres, and some guy said something that sounded like: "Welcome to ah fayuh city. Ahd lahyik to tell you folks how glad ah am y'all could come visit us." Though I'd been to Charlotte before, my ear couldn't adjust to this Southern speech, and most of the time, I didn't understand what was being said.

Jack was a big promoter, but we soon saw he was not a wasteful spender. Our next stop after the airport reception was a little cocktail party at his French–Swiss Ski College, and he packed along the same hors d'oeuvres he had served at the airport. His ski school was at a little ski area called Appalachian Ski Mountain. When we got there, he explained to everyone that the French–Swiss Ski College had the exclusive contract with West Point to teach the aspiring army officers to ski, and he claimed he got this contract because he had invented a top secret ski turn to be performed by ski troops.

"You ski along at fifty miles an hour with a rifle and a field pack," he told us. "Then you do this special movement I've invented; that permits you to stop immediately and fire your rifle. I can't explain how it's done because it's still classified Top Secret. Only the Green Berets have been taught how to do it."

Now, as a matter of fact, Jack did have a contract to teach West Pointers how to ski. I guess he got it just because he's a shrewd promoter. But this tale of his special stop and turn had all of us laughing. As for the reporters, I suspect they knew you had to take Jack with a grain of salt. He claimed to have been Marilyn Monroe's press agent (I think that was true, though with Jack you never know). The previous year, he had tried to get a police escort for me when we drove from Charlotte to Boone. The police turned him down so he kept calling ahead to the next town to tell the police we were lost, and at each town there would be an escort waiting.

For all his press agentry, he took good care of us, setting us up in excellent chalets at Beach. We went there after going to his area, and again there was a cocktail party—and sure enough, the same hors d'oeuvres reappeared. Thereafter, though, the food in our chalet was superb—because Danièle cooked for us, which was certainly a great relief after all the motel food we had been consuming.

After Dr. Fee's comments, I thought Danièle might run into some problems shopping. Apparently, whatever deficiencies there are in the American diet do not start in the marketplace. Danièle was able to find fresh vegetables, meats, poultry—all the ingredients she needed for some really delicious soups. Soup is to the French housewife what chopped beef is to the American housewife. It's maybe even more of a staple. Many French homes have a pot of soup constantly on the stove. Vegetables, meat juicies, and various leftovers are constantly added. The French homemaker takes special pride in the soup recipes she can devise. Always with fresh ingredients, though. Soup to an American seems to mean opening a can and maybe adding another can of cold water. The French stomach can't abide the canned flavors Americans accept as a matter of course. Soup to a Frenchman is the delicious aroma of the fresh vegetables simmering in meat stock to just the right consistency. The liquid, whether clear or thick, is a guessing game of flavors, a meal in itself, or an appetite-arousing beginning to a sumptuous feast—literally, from soup to nuts.

It was perhaps this respite of good wholesome French cooking that emphasized for us again how tough it is for a competitor to be away from his home milieu. I recall a conversation I had with Michel about Spider Sabich. I commented that seeing how Sabich had developed, I thought he had made a mistake quitting the amateurs when he did.

"No," Michel said, "I disagree. If Spider had been a European, you'd be right. With his talent, if he had been a German or an Italian, he might have done very well on the World Cup circuit. But an American going to Europe has too many problems to overcome. Spider was certainly right to turn pro."

As the season wore on and I saw more and more what the problems could be for a racer competing on foreign territory all the time, I realized Michel was right.

Danièle didn't cook all our meals at Beach Mountain, of course, but my recollection of all the food I ate there is favorable. Jack Lester took us to some restaurants that were outstanding. Perhaps the cuisine was particularly good or perhaps Danièle's soups restored our palates. Anyway, we ate well.

It was just as well that Jack Lester was around to buoy up our spirits because the weather in North Carolina wasn't too promising. As we had expected, it was warm, but when it rained on Thursday, we had to cancel our skiing practice entirely. Jack arranged for us to play indoor tennis, and we cracked jokes about how Saturday's and Sunday's races would have to be run on an indoor course like tennis matches.

The race organizers, however, didn't appear to be too worried. "Nothing to be afraid of," one of them said. "There's a cold spell coming this way, and when it hits, we'll just make some snow."

Well, that's what happened. It turned bitter cold. The day of the giant slalom was twenty-two degrees below zero on the wind-chill scale. We had warm weather in Canada and Minnesota, where everyone told us to be prepared for the cold, and down here where we should have had the warm weather, the bottom fell out of the thermometer. What a crazy winter!

Though the snow was artificial, there was nothing artificial about the mountain. The summit is over 5,500 feet above sea level, higher than most of the mountains in New England. But only the top part is used for skiing; thus, the vertical is only 800 feet. That high up, the Southern skies do occasionally drop snow, but snow guns provide most of the skiing.

The course was fairly interesting, containing an unusual dog-leg to the left. I had the best qualifying time in the giant slalom, then went on to beat Peter Duncan in the opening round, Doug Woodcock in the quarterfinals, Dan Mooney in the semifinals, and Hugo Nindl in the championship round.

There was now no question that I was back on my skis. It was clear I understood the pro format well enough and that I could win. The only remaining question was whether I could win consistently. And could I win at slalom?

The answer on Sunday was not promising. I made it as far as the semifinals, where I lost to Otto Tschudi. Otto was skiing very well—he went on to win against Sabich—but I could see now that I just hadn't prepared sufficiently to build up my stamina. Perhaps if I had done more long distance running in the summer, I would have been better prepared to handle running nine courses two days in a row.

Only racers who have experienced this routine can appreciate how tiring it can be. Michel, for instance, was baffled, "I can see you're tired," he'd say, "but I don't understand what the problem is. You win at giant slalom, and then you get the best qualifying time in slalom, so it has nothing to do with the format of the race, or your ability to run slalom. Yet, these are such short runs, I don't see why you should be so tired from them."

"You'd understand if you tried it," I told him. I have to admit, if I hadn't been doing it myself, I don't think I could have understood how tiring it could be because the courses certainly didn't look that demanding. But there's no question it's tough. Not just physically, but mentally, too. Sometimes on the second day, I would really feel it in my legs. Usually, though, what would go first was my concentration. And then I would make a foolish mistake like dropping my poles or skating too wide or looking at the other guy to see how he was doing. These things happened to me more in slalom than in giant slalom simply because the slalom was always the second day and I was tired. These lapses in concentration were no doubt due in part to my long layoff and failure to get my mind properly attuned to the competitive situation. But mostly they were simply signs of fatigue.

Michel, however, kept looking to see whether my equipment could be playing a role. He was convinced that I still didn't have the right ski for slalom.

In the other semifinal that day, Stuefer faced Sabich—and a peculiar thing happened. One of the slalom poles on Stuefer's course had been knocked down and the gatekeeper set it up so that it was leaning in toward the other slalom pole of that gate. This penalizes the skier who has to come through the gate because he can't pass as close to the pole as he could if it were in the snow perpendicular to the slope. In effect, that's what happened to Stuefer. The flag was blocking his line and he had to bend and pass around and under it.

Stuefer protested, but the course referee was at the bottom and couldn't see the offending pole. As for the gatekeeper, either he didn't know what it was all about or else he didn't want to admit he had done something wrong. At any rate, Stuefer's protest wasn't allowed. From the way he was skiing, I'm convinced he would have beaten Sabich if that pole had been in straight.

So instead of facing Tschudi in the championship round, Stuefer raced against me in the consolation round. And it was unbelievable. It almost seemed as though the gatekeeper were trying to make amends for having cheated Stuefer in the preceding round, for suddenly, I found a pole leaning over on my course, forcing me to lose time just as it had Stuefer in the preceding round. Again the referee claimed he didn't see it, and again the gatekeeper played dumb. I felt certain I'd have beaten Stuefer if I hadn't lost those precious moments ducking around that leaning slalom pole. The difference between third and fourth place is five points and $200. In Stuefer's case, it might have been the difference between third and first place, or ten points and $1,300. When I left Beach Mountain still in third place behind Sabich and Stuefer (though I was now in second place in earnings), I was beginning to think that this professional racing circuit could stand a bit more professionalism.

8
MICHIGAN DRAMA

I WAS now more than halfway through the pro racing schedule. I was in contention for the Grand Prix, a threat, always in position to overtake the leaders, Sabich and Stuefer, if they should falter. But that wasn't where I wanted to be. Some competitors like to come from behind, feeling they do best when they have something to shoot for. In amateur slalom racing, for example, many competitors say they prefer to be second or third after the first run, within hailing distance of the leader, but without having the pressure of knowing everyone is gunning for you.

Not me—I prefer to be first. Let the other guys try to overtake me. I figure the pressure is on them. If, in the second run, another skier has just as good a time as I have, I still win if I had the best time in the first run. By the same reasoning, on this pro tour, I'd rather have been out front. Maybe it made Sabich and Stuefer nervous to look over their shoulders knowing I was creeping up in third place. But they'd have been still more nervous if I'd had the lead and they had to try to catch up.

Danièle suggested that maybe I'd been trying too hard, that maybe I needed a rest. Mark McCormack was at Arnold Palmer's golf course, the Bay Hill Country Club in Orlando, Florida, and invited us to come down there for a short break. Peter Duncan, a Canadian skier who was an excellent golfer, joined us, and it was indeed a welcome respite.

The two days at Orlando were just enough to warm up my

spirits, not only from the sun and the beautiful golf course, but also to be away from the snow for awhile. We visited Disney World and felt just like kids—no cares, just having fun. Peter Duncan, who is about a four handicap golfer, helped my game, and when I headed for the next race, at Boyne, Michigan, it was as though I'd been away on a long vacation.

Right after the Boyne race, I was going to have to return to Florida for a sort of professional Olympics called the Superstar competition. This was to be held at Rotonda West, just outside of Sarasota. Because I'd be coming back south in less than a week, Danièle decided to stay in Florida while I went back north. She had some friends in Palm Beach—Margarette and Stanley Rumbough—and she went to visit them. Danièle and Margarette had been friends before Margarette's marriage. Her husband is a financier whose first wife was the actress Dina Merrill (a son of theirs was killed in a sailing accident in the late summer of 1973). The plan was for the Rumboughs to bring Danièle up to Rotonda when I went there to compete the following week.

I had never visited Boyne before. I knew that Othmar Schneider, a one-time great champion for Austria, was head of the ski school there. During my association with General Motors, people from Detroit were always asking me if I had been to Boyne and what I thought of it, but until now, I had never had the opportunity to see it—or ski it.

I could see why these auto executives from Detroit talked so much about it. Located in northern Michigan, the area consists of a picturesque village situated at the base of a broad, steep ridge. The runs are short, but there's a lot of variety and an amazing complex of lifts—three- and four-place chair lifts, for example. The base lodge is a big building with a clock tower, restaurant, and all the amenities skiers look for.

There was a party for us when I got there and I met the owner, Everett Kircher. Othmar Schneider, who I knew from Portillo, Chile, where he used to run the ski school and whom I was looking forward to seeing again, was ailing with a bad back and couldn't be there.

Despite the overall impression that this was a deluxe establishment, my first night was miserable. My room was near the air compressors they use for making snow, and the noise sounded like my head was stuck in a giant turbine engine. I couldn't sleep at all. I complained and asked to have my room changed, but I was told that they had made all the snow they were going to need and the compressors wouldn't be running any more. They were true to their word, and after that, I slept soundly.

While I was in Florida, Michel had received a new batch of slalom skis from Rossignol and had mounted up about ten pairs to test. He was still convinced that my troubles on Sunday came as much from equipment as from fatigue. Anyway, while he was working on these test pairs, a guy from the Hart ski team came by and said he wasn't happy with his skis. "Can I try a pair of Jean-Claude's castoffs?" he wanted to know.

Michel shrugged, thought a moment, and decided he'd let the guy have a pair that he thought were probably the worst of the lot. The guy put them on his shoulder and started out to mount the bindings for his boots. Suddenly Michel changed his mind.

"No, I don't think I'd better let you have these yet," he said. "I think Jean-Claude had better try them first."

They were a pair of Stratos, a model Rossignol has had in its line for many years; most of the other skis he had selected were the newer ST 650s. Well, on February 15, when I tried these skis out, this was the pair I liked best. And Michel agreed that finally we'd found a pair that should work well for me. As it turned out, these were the skis that I was to use for the balance of the season. And Michel had almost given them away!

The race course at Boyne was the best prepared we had seen all season. The snow had been very carefully groomed; the gates were set more interestingly than we had seen so far; and the bumps were bigger than usual—all on a course that was both steeper and wider than any we had raced on till then. Having shown at Mt. Snow and Buck Hill that I could be the fastest on a flat course, I was anxious to do well here to prove that I hadn't lost my touch on the steep.

The qualifying round for the slalom was held on Friday, February 16. This was the first time it had been done this way. Usually, the qualifying round for the giant slalom is held first, and the qualifying round for the slalom is run on Sunday morning. I'm not sure why it was changed in this case, but it didn't matter to me. I did well enough, although I was on my edges a bit too much. I think I was still not used to the new Stratos. The big surprise was that Spider Sabich failed to qualify. This was the first time since he became a pro—in other words, the first time in fifty races spanning two and a half seasons—that Spider had failed to qualify for an event. It was an indication of Spider's unusual consistency that his failure to qualify had everyone talking. Only Stuefer and I had qualified in every event this season—but we didn't have Spider's record of two years of making the cut in every event.

For me, of course, Spider's failure meant an opportunity to take the lead. If I did well in the slalom and also in the giant slalom, I would overtake Spider. And, since only seven points separated Stuefer and me, I could also overtake Harald and leave Boyne in first place. It was quite an incentive, and I was determined to go out and do it.

On Saturday, for the giant slalom, Sabich succeeded in qualifying. That made the giant slalom his fifty-first successive race in the money—even though his string of successful qualifying runs was halted at fifty. This situation was peculiar because the slalom race, which was to be run after the giant slalom, had its qualifying run first. Knowing that he couldn't gain any points the next day, the pressure was on Spider to go all out. And, in fact, he skied very well, making it into the championship round. This was what the promoters had been waiting for all season, for I, too, made it into the finals. This was the first time that Spider and I faced each other in the championship round.

As I've explained, the course officials try to make the side-by-side courses identical. This is almost impossible to do, however. Though the gates can be carefully measured to be at the same angles and same distances and the bumps built in as nearly the same way as possible, the snow can never be identical on the two courses. The sun will strike one course differently from the way it strikes the other course. And the terrain itself is bound to have minor differences in pitch.

The courses are color coded to distinguish them: one is always green, the other gold. And the word soon gets around that the green is faster or the gold, as the case may be. If the difference gets to be too noticeable, the race officials will make an adjustment in one course or the other and announce what they've done to equalize them.

On this day, everyone was saying that the green course was both faster and tougher. What made it more difficult was a patch of ice just above the second jump. Once you cleared that jump, you could accelerate on the steep portion of the course and then carry speed across the flat section to the finish line.

In my first run against Spider, I drew the green course. I skied cautiously until I had passed the difficult section, then zipped on to edge Spider by a margin of .05 of a second. It was not a safe margin. The gold course, which I would race on for the second run, was not as fast. If Spider went all out, as I expected he would, I would have a tough time beating him. And if he came in first in the giant slalom, even if I took a first in the slalom the next day, the best I could do would be to come away from Boyne tied with him for first. So I realized I was going to have to give it everything on this run, really pour it on.

If the pressure was on me, it was on Spider even more. If he didn't beat me in this race, I could tie him by doing no better than third in the slalom. Maybe he wasn't even thinking about the next day, but he was surely trying hard. He wasn't as careful as I had been in the top part of the course and tried to take it straight coming off that tricky second bump. Out of the corner of my eye, I saw him fall—and I coasted on to my third straight giant slalom victory.

I felt pretty good about that, of course, but I had yet to get a first in slalom, so I was anything but overconfident next day. In my opening round on Sunday, I faced the American, Hank Kashiwa. Kashiwa was turning out to be an enigma for many people. He had shown promise as an amateur but never rose to the top. After Sapporo, where, because of his Japanese–American parentage he was something of a local favorite, he turned pro and took a first in the first race he entered. This season, after some fairly good early results, he was doing nothing. Yet, he seemed to be skiing well.

I think if Kashiwa had been working with somebody like Michel, he might have discovered what the problem was. The big difference between the approach Michel and I took and what seemed to be the attitude of the others is that we insisted on getting the last inch of performance out of every piece of equipment. We experimented and worked at it constantly till we were sure there wasn't a fraction of a second being lost because of some fault in the gear. More than that, Michel was always looking to push the equipment even farther, to make design changes that would give us a still greater advantage.

During my race against Kashiwa, it was apparent we had found the right slalom skis at last. At least for the snow we encountered at Boyne, these Stratos were performing like magic. Michel was ecstatic.

"This time, you're going to go all the way and finally win a slalom," he predicted.

I was just as optimistic. Everything felt right, and I knew with Sabich out of the race, this was my chance to take the lead in the overall classification. A win in slalom now would psych out the field. If I could put together back-to-back victories, I had the feeling this would demoralize the rest of the racers. After that, they'd feel I was invincible.

In the quarterfinals, I faced Alain Penz. After having been ill, Alain was coming back strong. He had never beaten me in any face-to-face match, and he resented it. If there was anyone who was out for blood when he raced me, it was Alain. And I knew how he felt, so there could be no let-up. I had to keep pressing if I was going to win this one.

All this time, a complicating factor put additional pressure on me. I was scheduled to fly to Sarasota, Florida, immediately after the race. A private plane was going to take me to Chicago where I was to get on another plane for Sarasota, and the Superstar Games. There was a lot at stake in the Superstars—potentially, I could make more there in two days than the $40,000 Grand Prix bonus for finishing first over the season, so I was anxious to get through here and fly on down to Florida.

From the top of the race course, I could see my chartered plane out there waiting for me. But I could also see something else: the clouds blowing in. A snowstorm was on its way, and if my plane was going to get safely off the ground, I should have been leaving instead of staying on to race.

Thus, as I faced Alain, I was in conflict. Should I deliberately go slow so I'd be out of the race, making sure that I'd get on the plane before the weather locked us in? Or should I try to win the slalom and trust that somehow I'd make it down to Florida for the competitions the next day?

Even though I wasn't sure it was in my best interest to try to win, I can't race not to win. It meant more to me than the money I might lose by not getting to the Superstars on time. So I ran two very tough courses—twenty-three gates each—to beat Alain and get into the semifinals.

That meant four more runs no matter how I did in the semifinals: two in the semifinals and two either in the championship round or the consolation round. At least there was no conflict here. Although I continued to keep one eye on the snowstorm that was now blowing in, there was no further question about my tactics. I had to give it everything.

My opponent in the semifinals was Hugo Nindl. I had faced Nindl in the final round in each of the last two giant slaloms I had won before Boyne. So I felt sure I could take his measure. In the other semifinal, Stuefer was facing Perry Thompson. If Stuefer won the final and I came in fourth again, I'd leave Boyne still in third place behind Sabich and Stuefer. I had to beat Nindl.

In the first run, I was ahead by .225 of a second. Not a very big lead, but I felt confident. The only thing was, all the tension of the afternoon was building up in my muscles and I was beginning to tire. Still, I couldn't believe it when I looked over in the other lane as I was nearing the finish line. Hugo was skating through the last gates with a clean advantage. He was .244 of a second faster than I was, which meant his combined time was .019 better than mine—a small margin but a big loss for me.

As badly as I wanted to win that race and as well as my skis were running that day, I just couldn't do it. I simply didn't have the stamina to ski seventeen runs in two days and win them all. Yes, I was distracted by the oncoming snowstorm and my waiting plane; but that merely added to the drama of the situation. I didn't lose to Nindl because of other things on my mind. It was simply fatigue.

In the run-off, I beat Perry Thompson for third place. So in effect, I did leave Boyne in first place in the overall standings —tied for first, that is, with Spider Sabich. In the finals of the Boyne slalom, Nindl beat Stuefer.

It was a curious race. Stuefer took the first heat by .134 of a second. Then, in the second run, Nindl fell going into the second bump. It looked like it was all over for him. But, great competitor that he is, he got back up, climbed a few steps so that he didn't miss his gate, and went on to finish the race. It was lucky for him that he did, because Stuefer fell just a split second later, right after the second bump. In his case, his fall caused him to miss a gate, leading to his disqualification.

Though I was now tied with Spider for first place in points, I was actually ahead of him in money winnings—$18,600 to $16,825. Had Stuefer taken a first, he would still have been third in the point standings, but he, too, would have been ahead of Spider on the money list. That was just a peculiarity of the scoring system.

A first and a third: Boyne was my best result to date. But I was disappointed. Until my second run against Nindl, I had felt certain I was going to end my stay at Boyne with a first and a first. That wasn't to be, though I was thoroughly exhausted from having made the attempt. And next day, I was going to be facing another kind of challenge. Later, there'd be a chance to rest. The next race was two weeks off—March 4 and 5 at Bear Valley, California.

My bags had been loaded on the chartered plane earlier in the day. It was already snowing heavily when I completed my racing for the day by beating Perry Thompson. Perry was racing very well that day but was demoralized by his semifinal battle with Stuefer. Stuefer had fallen coming off the second bump, but managed to get up without missing a gate. Thompson saw

Stuefer fall, thought he was out of the race, and proceeded to ski off the course.

At first, the officials ruled that Stuefer was disqualified for interference. Later they decided it was Thompson who should be disqualified for failing to complete the course. It was a tough decision for Perry, but I had no time to commiserate. After beating him, I went almost at a dead run to the plane. Michel came with me, for he was going back to France until the Bear Valley race and also had a plane to catch in Chicago.

I didn't know what was in store for me at this Superstar event. I was sort of a last-minute fill-in. I think originally Willie Shoemaker was supposed to be there, and then when he declined, Gary Player was going to substitute for him. When Gary couldn't make it either, they took me. I think I heard about it just before I left Geneva for Mt. Snow.

Anyway, I traveled half the night—it was two in the morning when I finally got down to Rotonda West—and I had to be up and ready to go at 8:30 the following morning. On a day following a weekend like this, I should have been resting. My muscles were all sore from pushing out of the starting gate so many times, taking all those jarring jumps, hitting the poles with my shoulders and knees, and trying so hard to win. Because the snow at Boyne had been so hard, with many icy sections, it meant I had to edge my skis more, and this, too, is harder on the muscles. I wasn't in much condition for any kind of competition, let alone one that was a test of general fitness.

I don't know how many people realize it, but the muscles you use in skiing are quite unlike the muscles you use for other sports. Or at any rate, you use them in a different way. Before a ski season starts, I'm generally a pretty fast runner and cyclist as a result of my pre-season conditioning program. Then, after skiing practically every day during the season, if I run or cycle again in the spring, I find I'm much slower. I don't claim to understand the physiology of this, but I do know that skiing is not a good way to train for other sports. It *is* a good exercise, a good general conditioner for the heart and lungs, but the muscle groups you develop while doing Alpine skiing train you only to do more skiing.

This may also be true of other sports. A guy who's in shape to play ice hockey isn't necessarily in shape to run or cycle or swim or lift weights. So I don't claim I was at any special disadvantage. I do know that I can be a lot better at the events I entered in the Superstar competition than I demonstrated at Rotonda. In any event, whatever handicap I was under because of coming right from a hard weekend of competition and getting only a half night's sleep, I had to make the best of it. There was a lot of money at stake, of course, but for guys of this caliber in sports—champions all—there was also a lot of ego involved. For my part, I thought it was a tremendous idea, and I was glad to be there, tired or not.

9
THE SUPERSTARS

I'VE ALWAYS been good at any sport I tried. This isn't true of all top athletes. I've mentioned Guy Périllat, for example, who was a superb skier, but who really didn't have the natural endowments to be a great sports figure. It makes his accomplishments all the more admirable, I believe.

But most of the French Ski Team members were good at a number of sports. If I happened to have been raised in a different part of France, I think I might have become a soccer player or a bicycle racer. No matter where I was raised, I would have been an athlete, and if I had been able to generate the same kind of dedication I gave to skiing, I believe I would have been just as successful at whatever sport I chose to specialize in.

I've known others with the same natural talents but who never achieved greatness in sports simply because of circumstances. When I was a boy, I had a friend whose father was a comptroller with a construction company that came to Val d'Isère to build the Tignes dam. The boy went to school with us, and I taught him how to ski. I think I showed him his first pair of skis and boots, explained where he should go to ski, showed him how to fix his bindings, how to turn, and so forth. Well, in a few years, he was winning school championships, skiing better than I was skiing at the time.

Unfortunately for him, his father moved to Lyons to take another job, and that was the end of his skiing. But he was a real natural at any sport. He took up biking, and two years later, he was the junior champion of Lyons which is tantamount to being national champion because the competition is very strong in that region. It indicated this kid was really talented —and versatile. I lost track of him after that, but I'm sure if he had had the opportunity to stay with any one sport, he'd have been a champion.

It may not be very modest of me to say so, but I feel that way about myself, too. Any sport I've ever taken up, I've been good at, and if I had spent the necessary time at it, there isn't one I couldn't have mastered at championship levels. I can't prove that, of course, because you can't relive your life. The sport I chose was skiing and that didn't allow me time for other sports. But I'm certain I could have been a championship cyclist or tennis player or whatever I took up.

What is it that makes a champion? I was born with a high capacity for nervous energy. Physically, I've never enjoyed very good health, but in our family, we are all very strong people, and I have great physical resistance, quick reflexes, good balance, agility, and resilience. I think there are probably many people who have such natural endowments. With training, you can develop those traits necessary for your sport; you can train either for quickness and sharpness—as in a sprint—or for strength, depth, and endurance. Anyone good at sports in general can develop a specialty through hard training.

The extra ingredient that makes the champion is mental. I think that I have fantastic determination, a willingness to win, an ability to concentrate only on winning. That's why I work harder than anyone I know when I train. It's not any physical gift that tells me I can succeed at any sport. It's the knowledge that championship performance comes from a winning attitude. And that I know I have.

The invitation to the Superstar event gave me a chance to see if I was right, to see whether I could be the best at any sport. Or rather, it would give me a chance to show how good I was at sports which were not mine compared to other champions also engaging in sports which were not theirs.

The idea is supposed to have originated with Dick Button.

He was an America figure skater who won an Olympic gold medal in 1948. He won an award that year as America's best amateur athlete, but he claims he was embarrassed by this accolade because he didn't think he was much of an all-around sportsman. So he dreamed up an idea for a special kind of decathlon to find out who the real champion athletes were. He never got it off the ground, though, until he presented it to the makers of Fram Oil Filters who agreed to underwrite half the sponsorship costs for an ABC-TV special. Actually, it was Trans World International, a division of International Management, that put the show together, and Rotonda West, a real estate development about forty miles from Sarasota, that co-sponsored it for the privilege of the national TV exposure it would get for hosting it.

The champions who were invited may not have been the ten best all-around athletes—not by a long shot. But they were certainly tops in their own sports. It appeared that they were selected to attract the biggest viewing audience. Sports that are popular on TV were important, and to broaden the appeal, it seemed wise to have as many sports represented as possible. There was also some attempt to get athletes from varied ethnic and racial backgrounds—again, presumably, to broaden the TV appeal.

As I mentioned, I was selected only after Willie Shoemaker, the jockey, and Gary Player, the golfer, were unable to appear. I assume the organizers reasoned more people watch horse racing and golf on TV than watch skiing. Or maybe, since IMC had a hand in the selections, they reasoned that I might not have the time because I was on the pro tour.

Anyway, I was glad that things worked out so that I could be there. The others included Peter Revson, the car racer; Joe Frazier, the former heavyweight boxing champion; Rod Gilbert, the New York Rangers hockey star; Bob Seagren, the gold medal Olympic pole vaulter; Jim Stefanich, the bowling champion; Johnny Bench, catcher for the Cincinnati Reds baseball team; Johnny Unitas, quarterback for the San Diego Chargers football team; Elvin Hayes, the six-foot-nine-inch basketball player for the Baltimore Bullets; and Rod Laver, the leading money winner on the pro tennis tour.

I was relieved to find I wasn't the only one who appeared there right out of a busy competitive schedule. The day before, Rod Laver had taken Roy Emerson in straight sets in Toronto. Hayes and Gilbert both came down smack in the middle of their seasons. The Rangers, in fact, had played Sunday night, and Gilbert arrived even later than I did, showing up at 7 A.M. Revson and Stefanich competed all year round in their specialties. Besides, Stefanich had been laid up with pneumonia two weeks before. Bench, too, wasn't long out of the hospital; he was still recuperating from lung surgery. Nevertheless, I do think I had had the most tiring weekend, the least amount of time to prepare for this contest, and possibly the least amount of sleep beforehand.

Even though I was fighting fatigue from the moment the events began, I was quite enthusiastic about my prospects. There were ten events and each competitor had to pick seven of the ten in which to compete. The only restriction was you were not allowed to pick your own sport. That didn't matter to me, of course, since skiing wasn't one of the sports included. The choices were among golf, tennis, swimming, bowling, weight lifting, hitting baseballs, table tennis, a 100-yard dash, a half-mile run, and a two-mile bike race.

In most of these events, I was quite strong. Baseball was out of the question for me, of course. We don't play that in France. I had bowled a few times, but that certainly wasn't a sport I felt proficient at. I wasn't too good at golf or tennis, either, so it was hard for me to decide which of these two I should include. I suppose my tennis game was the stronger, though I knew I wasn't very good.

But I had recently taken up golf and enjoyed it very much. So I decided to compete in it and forego tennis—and that turned out to be a terrible mistake. I was a 24-handicap golfer; many of the others were scratch players—I mean real scratch. On the other hand, most of the tennis players were terrible, and I'm sure that with any luck in the draw, I could have scored well in that.

Both money and points were awarded for each event: the winner got $3,000 and ten points; second place was worth $2,100 and seven points; third earned $1,200 and four points; fourth earned $600 and two points; and fifth earned $300 and one point. The overall point winner would get an additional $25,000; the second place finisher overall would get a $15,000 bonus; and the third place finisher would collect another $10,000. On top of all this, each of us was given a quarter-acre plot of land in the Rotonda West development—said to be worth about $9,000 each. So there was a chance to walk away with a lot of money as well as a lot of glory. Despite my fatigue, I was keyed up to do my best.

The first event was tennis, and I immediately regretted my decision to sit this one out. I don't remember when I've seen worse playing. Jim Stefanich served seven straight faults. It was no wonder: it was the first time he had ever played. Elvin Hayes and Johnny Unitas weren't much better. Bob Seagren, who turned out to be a really fantastic athlete, played a creditable game, but Revson, who won, and Gilbert looked like the only ones who would have given me problems.

The next event was golf—and there was a fairly good crowd there to watch, much to my distress. I finished last. I got into a sand trap on the fifth hole and ended up with a 55—19 over par on this nine-hole course. Stefanich was first with a 41.

Swimming was next. It started out with fifty-meter qualification heats, with the five fastest racing 100 meters in the final. I swam very well. In my heat, I raced against Revson and Seagren and I won. In fact, it was the fastest time, overall, with Revson and Seagren getting the next fastest times. But then we had to go into the finals right away, and I was too tired. I couldn't even lift my arms. Revson came from behind to beat Seagren, and I came in a poor third.

I did better than Joe Frazier, though. He was *dog paddling* just to stay afloat and ended up walking on the bottom of the pool.

"It was like I was throwing punches at the water and the water kept hitting back," Frazier said. "My aim was to keep from drowning." He was very funny. When he dove in, he hit the water flat and made a tremendous splash. But he took it all with good humor. He came down only to have fun, he said.

My aim was higher, and I was particularly disappointed

because I felt sure that with sufficient rest, I would have beaten these guys in swimming. It's one of my better sports. In the afternoon, there was bowling, in which I didn't compete. And then came the weight lifting. Everyone thought Joe Frazier would take this, but he didn't know how to hold a barbell. Bob Seagren lifted 170 pounds to beat him. I came in third, which, considering my size, was pretty good.

That night, Danièle came up with the Rumboughs, and we had a relaxing, pleasant evening. But I was way down the list on total points, and we all agreed, that was impermissible. I just couldn't accept being that far behind and I decided to do something about it. So the next morning, I went into the events with a changed attitude. My fatigue was gone, and though I was way down the list, I wasn't going to let that depress me. I approached the final events very positively. The preceding day's debacle I set down to poor judgment in selecting golf over tennis and to fatigue in the swimming. Now I had had a good night's sleep, and events coming up—running, biking, and table tennis—were all things I should be able to do well at.

Seagren surprised everyone by winning the baseball batting contest. It was thought that either Gilbert or Hayes would win that (Bench, of course, was not allowed to compete). Then it was table tennis. I haven't played that enough to be good at it, but if the others played this the way they played tennis, I figured my chances were good. Actually, there were a couple of pretty good players, but through the luck of the draw, they met Rod Laver. I made it into the finals before I had to face him. Rod's game, they ruled, was tennis, not table tennis; but he outclassed us all. Of course, he killed me, beating me 11–0. Still that second place was encouraging.

In the 100-yard dash, I was up against a lot of men who did a great deal of running in their sports: Johnny Unitas, Elvin Hayes, Rod Laver, and others. But they were not as used to jumping out of a starting gate as I was. My body was very attuned to the starter's signal. And I had a great start. I realized I was ahead and I realized, too, that all these stadium athletes were fast and that it would be hard for me to stay ahead.

On my right side, I could hear Elvin Hayes and his tremendous stride. There were my legs going *tac-tac-tac-tac* as fast as I could pump them. And behind me I could hear this *PLOMP! PLOMP! PLOMP! PLOMP!*—this big man with his big legs drawing up on me. I felt like I was in a movie cartoon. I was the tiny little mouse being overtaken by this great big cat. And sure enough, he beat me right at the finish line. The time was 11.5 seconds—not exactly a new world record.

The half-mile run was next, and suddenly I realized I was in contention for second place overall. Peter Revson was the man I had to beat, so in this race, with Bob Seagren taking an early lead followed by Hayes, I just stayed with Peter Revson. A half mile is not a long-distance race, but in view of my record this season of running out of steam on the second day of competition, I was worried I might not be able to last. In effect, this was my fourth straight day of competition. I stayed with Peter Revson all the way, and at the end I had enough left in reserve to pass him and come in third.

That left only bicycle racing, and my chances for walking off with some prize money were looking very good. Rod Laver was competing in this event, and he had never used a bike with gears before. I showed him how to shift—actually, I showed him how to put it into the highest gear and I told him to leave it there as he wouldn't need a lower ratio. These were three-speed Columbia bikes, not the ten-speed racing bikes I was used to, but I figured I'd do well. At least I wouldn't have to worry about a novice like Laver.

At the gun, Seagren took off and Frazier took off with him. Well, I knew Frazier had no reason to be a good bicycle rider, so I didn't panic. There was no chance of my catching Seagren in any event—he was way ahead in the overall tabulation. Again, all I had to do was beat Revson. But I was slowed down watching Frazier. He was pedaling away like mad, and I was laughing on my bike because I knew he couldn't last long. And, of course, he didn't. He developed muscle cramps in his thighs and had to stop.

There were one-mile qualification heats followed by a two-mile final. All I had to do was beat Revson, and I would win the second-place money. Still, I wanted to do better than just beat Revson. For my training the previous summer, I had done quite a lot of cycling. In fact, I've always been a strong cyclist and I expected to do very well in this event.

What I had forgotten is that biking requires constant work. At the beginning of my summer training, I'd find that after a couple of miles of cycling, I'd be exhausted. By the end of the summer, I'd be going for 100 kilometers or more at top speed, and if I was out with a group, we'd be fighting for the lead the whole way. But then, after a season of skiing, even though I had stayed in shape, I didn't have it for biking any more. I'd have to start all over again.

That's the way it was down at Rotonda. I just didn't have it to battle Seagren. Instead, I stayed back with Laver the whole way, in position to take second in this event and also a second overall. But just before the finish line, Laver surprised me and sprinted ahead. He was the one to take second, and I came in third. Probably, if I hadn't told Rod how to use his gears, I'd have beaten him. But it didn't make much difference. He needed more than a second in this race to beat me overall, and with my third, I had enough to beat out Revson.

In total money, Seagren walked off with $39,700. I got $23,400; and Revson and Laver each won $13,100. That wasn't bad for two days of competition.

The developer of Rotonda was the Cavanagh Communities Corporation whose vice-president was the TV announcer Ed McMahon. It was at a dinner he gave in his freshly finished house that we were all given our quarter-acre lots. Some of the journalists complained that the whole atmosphere surrounding the events was overly commercial. I suppose it *was* a field day for the hucksters. But it was a field day for us, too. And I think for the television audience that watched it all the following week.

Interestingly enough, all the top winners—Seagren, myself, Revson, and Laver—came from individual sports rather than team sports. I found that rather revealing. It wasn't that we were in better shape than the baseball player, football player, basketball player, or hockey player. Seagren was certainly in better all-around shape than any of us, but otherwise I don't think conditioning explains the results. I think the team-sport man has a different kind of drive. His ego involvement is not the same. Johnny Unitas openly admitted he had come down for the fun of it. Frazier said that, too, which may explain his poor showing, though he is not a team-sport man.

For myself, I know I just can't accept the idea of losing. Sure, there was a lot of money at stake, but the only one to whom that kind of money looked enormous was Bob Seagren, who had been an amateur up to that point. For the rest of us, it was a chance for a good payday, but as Peter Revson kept telling Seagren, "You know, Bob, I race every weekend for $100,000. This is just pocket change for me."

I wouldn't say it was just pocket change to me. But I would have tried just as hard if there had been no money involved. Obviously, it isn't a matter of my reputation. Nobody expected me to be good at anything except skiing. Nobody, that is, except me. There's something inside me that gets working as soon as I'm involved in any competitive situation. It won't let me accept defeat. And I think it must be the same for anyone successful at any individual sport. You're on your own and only your own effort will show what you can do. And so you do it.

I think this Superstar idea is simply fantastic, and I expect to see it grow. If it's really to win acceptance as a sort of professional Olympics, or more accurately, a professional decathlon, the rules will have to change. I suppose it makes sense to ban a man from competing in his own sport if you want to find out who's the best all-around athlete. But then, it doesn't make sense to allow a tennis player to play table tennis any more than you'd allow a 100-yard dash champion to compete in a 220-yard dash. It may be a different event, but it's not a different sport.

I understand that they've now substituted an obstacle course for table tennis, which takes care of this objection. But I think a more sensible approach might be to select the competitors and the events on the basis of how many adults play the sport, which could be as interesting as selecting them on the basis of how many watch. The latter was approximately the idea at Rotonda, even if it wasn't expressly put that way. On a worldwide basis, this would probably mean including skiing, but very few team sports. If spectators are what you're after, then soccer and horse racing would have to be included, but maybe not bowling. Anyway, the basis of deciding which competitors to invite is not crucial. With qualifying rounds, as it is now set up, a large enough number of athletes can be invited to insure that all major sports are represented.

What is important is that the ten events include one from each of the sports represented by the competitors. Otherwise, the competitor whose sport is included is penalized. I could choose seven events out of ten. Rod Laver could choose only seven out of nine. Then, possibly as a special attraction, the winner of the event could face the athlete whose sport it is, with special bonus points if he beats the other guy at his own game.

The format will certainly change. Already, as I've noted, there are now qualification rounds. Interestingly, Karl Schranz, Spider Sabich, and Billy Kidd took part in one of them, but only Schranz qualified, coming in second. I was ill at the time, so I missed the opportunity to take on my old rivals in nonskiing competition.

In my view, the biggest problem remains the choice of sports, and substituting an obstacle course for table tennis is not the solution. The competitions should be related to the sports represented by those invited. But how do you test how well a guy is at a team sport? For baseball, we had the chance to bat against a mechanical pitcher, with the hitters being scored for distance. Yet, in a team sport like baseball, the top star might be a pitcher who can't hit at all, and a very valuable player might be an excellent fielder or even a hitter who is good at placement but not at distance. Similarly, if you tried to have individual contests for basketball—let's say shooting baskets—it doesn't necessarily test the skill of the most valuable man on the court, who might be the one who sets up the plays.

Since it would be very difficult to set up a valid test for the skill of a team sport and because I don't believe team sports players are apt to do well anyway, I would eliminate them from the competition.

What about skiing? Well, it's hard to hold such a competition in the mountains, so it would be hard to include skiing on snow as one of the categories. A slalom course on roller skis might be a solution. I'd be glad to face anyone who won that event.

10
CELEBRITY RACE

I GOT a big boost from the notoriety—and the money—I won at Rotonda. I would have liked to just stay down in Florida and relax in the sun till my next race at Bear Valley, but my schedule was full. Right after the Superstars, Danièle and I flew up to Vermont to film a commercial for the Berol Pen people at Bolton Valley, a small ski area outside of Burlington. In the commercial, the Berol people say there are 14,000 glass beads in the tip of their pens that make the pen track on paper like skis in powder snow.

I found the whole concept of 14,000 glass beads in a pen tip rather funny. The snow was good at Bolton, so the cameramen had no difficulty shooting footage for their analogy. But they wanted to film in the sunshine with blue sky. So we waited around for the sun. It never did come out, which made me regret all the more having to leave Florida so soon.

From Bolton, I flew to Denver to spend three days at the Breckenridge ski area to meet real estate people. I had signed a contract with Breckenridge where I was used in their ads saying I had a condominium there. As part of the agreement, I was to spend a certain amount of time at the condominium each year. It wasn't much time and it was a luxurious condominium, so it was all very pleasant.

But now I needed a sort of home base from which to operate while on the pro circuit. Not just me, but the whole Rossignol team. So I wanted to explore the possibilities of Breckenridge becoming such a base for us.

From Breckenridge, we flew to Sacramento, California, where we had arranged to meet Rod Laver and his wife Mary. They had agreed to come spend a week with Danièle and me at the next stop on the tour, Bear Valley. Mary Laver was a very good skier, but Rod didn't dare ski very much because of a bad back. He didn't want to risk injuring it further and thus endangering his ability to play tennis.

Rod had ascertained that there were bubble-covered tennis courts at Bear Valley before he agreed to come along. Bear Valley is in the Sierras not far from Lake Tahoe, so I figured if he got bored, he could always go over to the Nevada gambling casinos for his amusement. Actually, Rod had quite a good time. He gave me some tennis lessons while we were there and I discovered he is not only one of the world's top tennis players, he is also one of the world's top tennis instructors.

If I had had that kind of instruction before I went to Rotonda, I would surely have entered the tennis matches instead of the golf competition, and quite possibly I would have won that event. Maybe I still wouldn't have beaten Seagren, but my second place wouldn't have had the notation that it was achieved without winning a single event.

Our drive up to Bear Valley was kind of funny—funny in retrospect anyway. At the time, it was kind of scary. We didn't know the roads very well and there were terrible rains, flooding the roads till they were covered with water hub-cap deep. We were alone, it was late at night, and there were no other cars on the road. A couple of times we lost the road completely. Several times we had to turn back after following the wrong road. Fortunately, there was lots of beer in the car, and after a while, what should have been tense moments turned out to be rather happy ones.

Michel and his wife Chantal also joined us at Bear. He had brought back some new slalom skis from France—some 207-cm Roc 550s, but I didn't like them as well as the Stratos I was already using. They weren't bad; just a little too quick-acting for me. Michel, by the way, plays a lot of tennis, and he was quite pleased when Rod asked him to play. When Michel would hit a good one, Rod wouldn't bother to hustle after it. He would just call out to Michel that it was a good shot. That made Michel feel pretty good, and later he commented, "See, I can even win some from Rod Laver."

We discussed our equipment problems with Rod and he explained how he, too, worked continually on improving his racket, frequently experimenting with the grip. He told us he used a wooden racket because he found he could control the ball better. He claimed that a ball would stay within the bounds of a wooden frame longer than it would in a metal frame. Because the ball would bounce out of a metal frame faster, Rod felt it gave him less control. Players who needed additional power, he said, preferred the metal rackets.

Rod told us about the beginning of professional tennis when the players would ride all day on a train, then play at night for $200, go to bed at 4 A.M., and do the same thing all over again the next day. Though the $2,500 for a first that we now get in pro skiing is nothing compared to what pro tennis players now get, it wasn't always that way. "It takes time to get there," Rod told us.

We were surprised in many ways by what greeted us at Bear Valley, one of California's newer ski areas. The first year it opened, Bear had an arrangement with the Club Méditerranée, and Guy Périllat was supposed to run the ski school. Later they started their Celebrity Pro–Am races, inviting skads of movie stars to come compete in teams with professional ski racers.

The idea was a good one for publicity. Big names attract crowds and they attract the press. This year's event was no exception. I must say, the advance ballyhoo was so good, I was surprised to find the area was so small. Bear Valley consists mainly of some vacation homes hidden tastefully among the trees, a couple of lodges, shops, restaurants, the tennis courts, and parking lots. The skiing is actually at Mt. Reba, about five miles away. Snow depths were astounding when we got there; all those flooded roads down in the valley meant snow up here —twelve to fifteen feet of it when we arrived. I had never

seen so much snow, but I understand this is normal—or almost
so. The Sierras are known for getting huge quantities of snow,
though not always of the best quality. Among American skiers,
"Sierra powder" is a euphemism for deep, heavy, wet snow
which sometimes seems to have the consistency of wet cement.

We stayed at the lodge, an elegant, carpeted edifice with nice
furnishings and good food. My old friend Jimmy Heuga had
been connected with the management here, and though he was
now otherwise employed, he was on hand to greet us. Ni
Orsi, another former racer with whom I had had so much fun
in 1964, was also around in some management capacity for
the development company.

I wasn't the only one of our *ménage* running into old friends.
There were many people from the movie colony here, and
Danièle enjoyed being in her element again. The Pro–Am
contest, sponsored by the Faberge cosmetics people, was
obviously very important to her, perhaps the highlight of our
tour.

The way that event worked, each racer was teamed with
some celebrity. The results were scored by team, that is, the
combined time of the racer and the celebrity. The teams were
supposed to have been selected by drawing lots, but someone
told me that Ethel Kennedy, the widow of the late Senator
Robert Kennedy, had insisted she be paired with me. That was
very flattering, but if Mrs. Kennedy pulled any political strings
to make us a team, I was unaware of it. What I was aware of
was the intense importance many of the stars seemed to place
on the race. Clint Eastwood, for example, prepared by hiring
three instructors—including Peter Brinkman, the ski school
director—to give him private lessons to help him improve his
technique. He was not a good skier even after his concentrated
lessons, but he tried hard.

I had met Mrs. Kennedy two years before at Waterville Valley,
New Hampshire, and skied with her then. The occasion was a
Head Ski promotion. The owner of Waterville Valley, Tom
Corcoran (a former Olympic racer), was a family friend of the
Kennedys, and Mrs. Kennedy skied at the area often—including
last year when she broke her leg. When I met her this time,

I said, "You know, Mrs. Kennedy, the Kennedy–Killy team has got to win." I wanted to give her some feeling of purpose, to get her to try hard. Otherwise, I figured we'd have no chance because some of the other combinations included some fairly good men skiers.

"I wouldn't be here if I didn't intend to win," she answered. I needn't have worried about her. She wanted to win so much, I think it's quite possible she specifically asked to ski as my partner, hoping that would improve her chances.

Ethel Kennedy was a very aggressive skier. She told me she had learned to ski at Lake Placid, New York, many years ago and had introduced her late husband to the sport. She was what you would call an advanced skier. What she lacked in form and technique, she made up in aggressiveness. She even complained to the race officials that the course was too easy. If her attitude carried over into the race, I figured we'd have a good chance.

Some of the Hollywood gossips at that time were saying that Andy Williams, the entertainer, would be Mrs. Kennedy's next husband. Mrs. Kennedy had the reputation of being a practicing Catholic, so it is doubtful that she would be considering marriage to a divorced man. In fact, Andy, an old family friend, wasn't even divorced. His wife was Claudine Longet. Anyway, over the weekend, everybody was friendly with everyone else, much to the consternation of the gossip columnists.

These know-it-all columnists were funny. One wrote that I had met Danièle on the set of Snow Job. I suspect that much of the rest of their commentary was equally accurate. But there did seem to be some effort by some of the celebrities to provide them with copy. Janet Leigh, the hostess for the event, dressed in very clingy clothes—she and Claudine Longet seemed to be vying with each other to see who could look the sexiest. They both succeeded admirably. Even Janet Leigh's teenage daughter, Jamie Curtis, a very flirtatious young thing, looked seductive.

Friday, the stars were all out practicing. They had to run a simple course to get a handicap time. Some of them seemed to be skiing slowly on purpose so that their handicaps would be bigger, thus improving their chances of winning. It was said that someone accused Claudine Longet of that, and she was furious. She was a good enough skier not to need that kind of advantage, but some women find the principles of sportsmanship hard to fathom.

Robert Stack, the Eliot Ness of TV, was there with his wife Rosemary, and I skied with him and arranged for him to get a pair of Rossignols. He was skiing on rented skis at Bear. When I called the Rossignol people and told them who the skis were for, they were quite excited. Stack is a hero in France because the Eliot Ness show is seen on French TV and is very big there.

Liza Minelli was also there, loking like she had just stepped off the set of *Cabaret*. She was going with Desi Arnaz, Jr., at the time, but also seemed to be quite friendly with Eddie Albert, Jr. Later, I understand, she started dating Albert.

The celebrity races were supposed to be run on Saturday and Sunday afternoons. But on Saturday afternoon, it suddenly started to snow again—a real Sierra storm—and that canceled the race. It came down so heavily, the roads were blocked, and the busses couldn't take the people back from Mt. Reba to Bear Valley. Rod was back at the area playing tennis (with Ethel Kennedy, I believe), but Mary Laver, Danièle, and I managed to ski back before things got too jammed.

Others congregated at the race headquarters hospitality suite trying to figure out how to get back to Bear Valley. Some made it back by snowmobile, some waited for the roads to be cleared, and some tried to make it back on skis—but as the afternoon wore on, that was not too wise. On top of everything else, there was a blackout when the electric power was cut.

That night, there was a big banquet to be followed by a fashion show, with Janet Leigh as hostess. We sat with the Lavers and went to bed early, missing a lot of excitement. First off, the storm kept raging outside, and after electric power was restored when an auxiliary power unit was thrown into service, it went out again, and part of the fashion show had to be given by candlelight.

There were a lot of stories about what happened to people stranded in the storm. Ethel Kennedy and her official escort, Frank Gifford, the ABC sports announcer, for example, found themselves in some couple's camper-trailer where at least they were lucky enough to get something to eat. They broiled steaks over a charcoal fire, drank beer, and played bridge well into the night. Mrs. Kennedy just loved it, she told me next day.

In the lodge, various unattached people found the blackout a fine excuse to get attached—or maybe it was the other way around. At any rate, there was much talk the next morning of amorous escapades spurred on by this feeling of "Maybe we'll never get out of here, so what the hell, why not?"

The biggest excitement, though, was the report that two small boys, sons of guests at the lodge, had been lost on the mountain. It was feared they had tried to ski back to Bear Valley from Mt. Reba and had fallen into one of the many ravines or just been buried in the deep snow. Even if they were just wandering around, this could be a terrible thing, for temperatures at night in the high mountains get very low, and even adults in such a predicament have died of exposure. When the word got out —during the fashion show, Robert Conrad, who was assisting Janet Leigh as commentator, was handed a note to announce that all sheriff's reservists were to report to the sheriff's office— there was a flood of volunteers to help the posse find the youngsters. Most of the celebrities who offered to help were turned down, though Conrad and Clint Eastwood, who have homes at Bear Valley and therefore knew the terrain, were allowed to assist.

Eddie Albert Jr. (star of *Butterflies Are Free*), who up to that point had been quite a cut-up, playing drums half the night with the lodge band, stayed up till dawn to help organize a rescue patrol. Bob Beattie helped round up a bunch of racers to take part in the hunt.

It was a problem getting around in that deep snow. Another eighteen inches had fallen during the storm. Only accomplished skiers could have participated in a man hunt under such conditions. But this was probably the most talented ski patrol party ever sent out to sweep an area anywhere. Helicopters were used to drop the racers onto the steep powder slopes and back bowls in the desperate search.

At dawn, we were blessed with a bright, cloudless sky so that visibility was perfect. Finally, at 9 A.M., a ski instructor—a Frenchman named Pierre David—found the kids. They had taken the wrong trail during the storm and realized they were lost. They were found near Bear Lake, where they had built an igloo shelter to protect them from the wind. They had used some of their down garments to help insulate the shelter, and then bedded down for the night. Wisely, they dug in on the flat, out of danger of slides. And wisely, too, they stayed put till they were rescued. According to David, they saw him and called out almost casually, "Hey man, you know the way back to Bear Valley? We been stuck here all night."

The search delayed the slalom on Sunday for two hours, but no one complained. The happy outcome left everyone feeling relieved.

It wasn't until Sunday afternoon that the Pro–Am race was held—on the easy NASTAR course at the area. By this time, the weather had changed again, and during the race, once again it started to snow. These were dual slalom courses, with the celebrities paired to race against one another, though the results were not based on who won in these heats, but rather on each individual's time minus his handicap (as computed against the time of a pacesetter who foreran the course) plus the time of the pro member of his team. The scoring was too complicated for spectators to comprehend, so these head-to-head contests seemed to matter, though they had little bearing on the final outcome.

Thus, Claudine Longet, in a good race between good skiers, beat Mary Laver. In another good race, Claudine's sister, Danièle, beat Janet Leigh. Robert Stack was faster than Lloyd Bridges, and Desi Arnaz, Jr., was faster than Beau Bridges.

Henry Mancini beat Clint Eastwood, but Henry's daughter Monica Mancini, was beaten by Jamie Curtis. Bob Conrad was another winner, beating Ben Murphy. I think Liza Minelli just watched, as did Merv Griffen, Ron Ely (he was the commentator), Tom Brokaw, Ginny Mancini, Angel Thompkins, and others. Ron Ely wanted to ski, but his studio was afraid a broken leg wouldn't look good on Tarzan.

Of course, Danièle won her race—she beat Frank Gifford, which made her feel pretty good. Frank is not only a sportscaster, but a former professional football player. And Ethel Kennedy, skiing better than I thought she would, won her match against Mrs. Otis Chandler, wife of the owner of the *Los Angeles Times*.

Danièle was teamed with Hugo Nindl and after her good result, anxiously awaited the performance of the pros. In the final standings, Mrs. Kennedy and I had the best combined time; Desi Arnaz Jr., teamed with Perry Thompson, came in second; and Danièle and Hugo came in third. When the results were announced, Danièle was in tears. She was just furious with me, and I couldn't understand why.

"This race didn't mean anything to you," she said. "It's no extra money, no extra points. You could have let me win here in front of all my friends."

I was dumbfounded. She had won her race and had skied very well. She could be proud of her performance and there was nothing she could do about how Hugo fared.

"But darling," I tried to explain, "even if I had snowplowed through the course, you and Hugo wouldn't have won. Desi Arnaz and Perry Thompson would have been the winners if Mrs. Kennedy and I hadn't won."

She couldn't understand this. I stayed in the doghouse until they gave her a cup for her third-place finish. With that kind of recognition in front of her friends, she was happy. As for me, I realized that even to make the woman I love happy, I couldn't allow myself to be beaten in a ski race. I suppose if I were racing just against Danièle, I could let her win. But then she would know it, and it wouldn't help. What finally consoled her was when I pointed out that her real time—before the handicap was added in—was one of the best among the amateurs.

The Bear Valley weekend included some serious racing, too. The qualifications for both giant slalom and slalom took place on Friday, March 2. The snow was poor—soft and easily cut up. After about the tenth racer had run, it was impossible. I had the best time on my course in the giant slalom, but in the slalom I had a poor draw and had to start about twentieth. By that time, the course was really rough. I never thought I'd be able to qualify. I had to go through such a mess of ruts, it seemed impossible that I would make it into the opening round. Still, I managed the second best time.

On Saturday, for the giant slalom, I ran against Anderl Molterer in the opening round. Every time I face him, I can't help marveling at how a man his age keeps in such fantastic shape. Out of forty racers in the qualification run, only sixteen make the cut. That means that Molterer, now well in his forties, had beaten two dozen guys who are half his age. Against such a fighter, I knew I couldn't let up. But I skied well and made it into the quarterfinals.

During the race, by the way, Rod Laver was walking up and down the side of the course to watch from different angles. I was amazed at how excited he was over the format. "This is great," he said. "No reason it shouldn't become just as big as pro tennis."

In the quarterfinals, I faced Malcolm Milne. Malcolm, who has a farm in Australia where he raises hops for beer, had been doing better on this circuit than anyone—himself included— had expected. He joined the tour as sort of a last fling before settling down to his farm business, and here he was in the top ten. But my skis responded just as I wanted them to, and I took Malcolm handily.

My opponent in the semifinals was Hugo Nindl. He had beaten me in the slalom semifinals at Boyne, so I had a score to settle with him. I don't mean this in any personal way. As a matter of fact, I like Hugo very much, I get along with him probably better than I do with any other racer on the circuit. Hugo was a great amateur when I was on the French team; if it hadn't been for injuries, he would probably have been a world champion. He and I and the other older racers— compared to the real youngsters, that is—share the same feelings about the sport, share some memories of races we had been in together, and thus understand one another and respect one another.

Still, it rankled me that he beat me at Boyne. Knowing that he was a dangerous competitor, I was determined that the same thing wouldn't happen here. Again I won.

In the other semifinal, Alain Penz faced a new man on the tour, Ed Reich. Reich was a young Austrian who had taught skiing at Vail and then shifted to Sun Valley. At Sun Valley, his racing talent was called to the attention of the area owner, Bill Janss (a former racer himself), who put Reich on a paid leave to let him try his luck as a pro. And here he was in his first race making it all the way to the semifinals. He could turn out to be a dark horse threat, I thought.

Despite uneasiness over new talents to contend with, I was pleased to see the pro tour was still attracting young racers. Terry Palmer, Tyler's younger brother, also joined the tour here. He was a member of the U.S. Ski Team and was considered the second best slalom expert the Americans had. There had apparently been some friction between him and his coaches, and as soon as he turned twenty-one, he quit the team to join the pros.

This could only be good for the pro league, for it was bound to spread the idea that ski for pay was the next logical step for a young racer who had made it to his national ski team. Interestingly, Terry added to the prestige of the tour by doing poorly. He didn't qualify in the giant slalom, and in the slalom, he was to lose to Alain Penz in the opening round. He was quoted in one newspaper as saying it "was a big shock to me. You don't realize it from the sidelines, but when you're in there, it moves. Those guys are about two seconds faster than you think. It's hard, very hard competition."

It was also hard for the Austrian, Ed Reich—too hard. So the finals were between Alain and me. Alain was still looking for his first victory against me in a head-to-head race. He made no bones about his jealousy. He resented my joining Team Rossignol. Prior to that, it was Penz who was the leading figure on the team, but, aside from the fact that there was more public interest in what Killy did than in what Penz did, for some time now, I was the one in contention for the Grand Prix, not Penz. And he was rankled by this.

Penz had always had a bad temper. Even as an amateur, he was not well liked by most of his teammates because of the way he would fly off the handle when he was crossed. Within the Rossignol team, the situation was aggravated because Michel and I have our own methods of work that did not coincide with what Penz thought the whole team should be doing.

With this undercurrent of friction between us, I knew Penz would be out to beat me if he possibly could. When I got into the starting gate, it had turned very cold and the visibility was poor. The big snowstorm was just starting. I turned around to see where Penz was. He was off in the woods, fixing his skis, wiping his goggles, and otherwise making it quite obvious that he was stalling. It looked to me like an attempt to psych me out.

"Do you want me to call Penz and tell him to get behind the gate?" the starter wanted to know.

"I don't care how long he takes," I said, loudly enough for him to hear. I figured two could play the game, and I would psych him by showing he couldn't make me nervous.

By the time Penz got into position, the snowstorm was in progress for real. The visibility, which was poor at the outset, had now gotten so bad you could barely see two to three gates ahead on the course. When the gates finally opened, I shot out, and within four or five gates, I had a half-gate lead. In that light, I guess it must have looked to Penz as though I were going to disappear down the mountain.

I don't know what he was thinking, of course, but it was obvious he panicked. As racer after racer goes down the same course, a groove is worn in the snow. It's tough to make good time skiing in that groove, but in a head-to-head race, it's the same for each man, so you just ski in the ruts as best you can. Well, when Penz saw me drawing ahead, instead of staying in the groove, he tried to cut it short. In a couple of gates, he was off the course.

Incidentally, by this time, the snow was coming down so heavy, the sensitive timing devices recorded a snowflake at the finish line. But in this race, a snowflake was the only thing that crossed the finish line before I did.

That made four giant slalom victories in a row, five victories in all—more than any of the other competitors. I was now in first place, but if Sabich could come back strong in the slalom the next day, I'd leave Bear Valley still tied. Spider had made it as far as the quarterfinals in the giant slalom, so in effect, I had to do at least as well to be tied for the lead when the Bear Valley races were over.

That was the night that, true to the Sierra reputation, it snowed a foot and a half. That meant an unusually soft course with deep ruts. My skis were too stiff for that kind of snow; I knew after the opening round, when I beat Ken Corrock, that I wasn't going to win. My skis carved too deeply into that soft surface. I tried to improve my chances by staying very close to the poles, but this is dangerous. For one thing, the slalom poles they use in the pros are much more solid, more unyielding, than the poles used in the amateurs. I remember, in my first pro race at Aspen, on top of all my other problems, I was black and blue all over from banging into those solid poles.

In the quarterfinals, I faced Perry Thompson, who was skiing very well. Coming off a jump, I slammed my left knee into a pole, badly jarring it, and soon after, I dug my ski into that soft snow and was out of the running.

Sabich, meantime, made it into the championship round against Terje Overland. If he won, he and I would still be sharing the lead. But despite the cheering of Claudine and other Hollywood friends, he lost his concentration briefly, and Terje beat him.

At last, I was in the lead.

11
DISASTER AND VICTORY

FROM Bear Valley, we went to San Francisco and in the morning I drove down to Monterey to see the Goodyear Tire people. They were down there shooting footage of Jackie Stewart; they wanted to talk to me about filming a commercial for their new snow tires. We reached an understanding, and then I drove back to San Francisco to pick up Danièle and meet Michel and his wife for dinner. We ate on Fisherman's Wharf in an excellent little restaurant where we ordered champagne to celebrate my being in first place.

The San Francisco area has a very European feel about it, in no small measure, I think, because of the number of fine restaurants one finds there. Small wonder so many Europeans say it is their favorite American city.

Next day, Michel and I met Barry Mackay, the former Davis Cup player, for some doubles at the San Francisco Country Club. Rod Laver, who was a friend of Mackay's, had set it up for us. Mackay and a friend of his who played with us were considerably better than we were, so it was more like tennis lessons than a tennis match, but very enjoyable for us nonetheless. We had lunch at the country club, too. It made for a very relaxing, pleasant interlude in the competitive schedule.

That afternoon, we flew to Salt Lake City and drove on to the Park City ski area where the next race was to be held. Danièle, meantime, had taken a plane home to Geneva, but

Michel's wife stayed and cooked for us all week, which once again, made life for us so much more pleasant.

I had been to Park City during the Killy Challenge, but that was four years before, and I was amazed to see how much it had grown. The resort is built around an old mining town, which is quite picturesque. The original aerial tram there wasn't designed for skiers at all; it carried lead, silver, and zinc from Treasure Mountain, as it is still called, down to an unloading building—the Silver King—that still towers over the town.

You can still see a lot of old mining equipment around Park City, and under the ski trails are several hundred miles of mine tunnels—long since inoperative. The mining theme dominates the decor of the buildings in town—old and new. But it's not over-done. Overall, the atmosphere is friendly and unmistakably American West. We stayed in one of the newer condominiums and found it comfortable—all in all, an enjoyable stay.

Until the race, that is.

Michel was still concerned that my equipment wasn't right. He had brought back some new Trappeur boot shells with him and we spent the next couple of days injecting the shells and comparing the new boots with the ones I had been using. The new shells were much stiffer and held my feet—the right one in particular—much better than the ones we had been using. We also continued to experiment with the 207-cm Roc 550 slalom skis, but I still didn't like the way they handled. I found that if I were too high after edging my skis in a turn, it would be too difficult to put them into a skid, to make them sideslip. Most of the time a racer wants to avoid skidding his skis, but there are occasions when you need to correct your line and a slight skid-ding movement is the easiest way to do it. These skis wanted to bite all the time.

Why this continuing search to improve my equipment? In pro racing, the secret of success is consistency. After years and years of running through slalom gates, my own reflexes pro-vided a good deal of consistency. By and large, I could count on them to give me predictable performance. But that was true only if my equipment could be counted on to respond in the same way to every input received from my legs and body.

Michel's objective was to guarantee that my equipment would respond as expected, to reduce the variables of the snow, the terrain—and me. It was demanding work on his part, but we both felt it was necessary.

My lead over Sabich at the start of the Park City races was only five points. And Stuefer, twenty-eight points behind, wasn't to be counted out either. It was still anybody's ball game. I was feeling confident, but I knew the season was far from over.

On Saturday, the day of the giant slalom, a few blue patches that were in the sky early in the day gave way to a uniform overcast gray. It looked as though a snowstorm might be developing. Utah is famous for its huge quantities of light, powdery snow. Unfortunately, what the tourist bureau forgets to mention is that you can't have all that powder snow without lots of stormy days. This looked like it was going to be a precursor of one of those days. The light was very flat. That is, the visibility was bad—not because of heavy fog, but because the grayish white day made it impossible to distinguish the contours of the terrain. There was no horizon, just a mass of white with the slope blending into the hazy sky. The temperature was up around forty degrees, which meant the snow was soft and would quickly become rutted.

On top of everything else, the course was difficult. There were twenty-seven gates, starting with a steep pitch, before the first jump. Then there were eleven more gates on a less steep section, followed by the second jump. Then four more gates, the third jump, and another four gates to the finish. It was probably the longest and certainly the most demanding course we had seen so far in the season.

As I believe I've explained, the qualification rounds are run against the clock, not man to man. They are run on the same dual courses, but you don't compete against the guy on the other course, only against the clock. The way it works is that those with the four best times on each course qualify. Then a second run is held, and again the top four on each course qualify. The order of running the qualifying round is determined by drawing lots.

In my first run, I was slow, with the fifth best time on my

course. I could blame the visibility or the soft snow, but it was the same for everyone. Perhaps I was just overconfident now that I was in first place. Or perhaps I was favoring my knee too much—it still hurt from hitting that pole at Bear Valley.

I had my concentration back on the second run, but this time, the light was so bad, I didn't see the second jump. I caught a tip and fell. For the first time in the season, *I had failed to qualify*. The only consolation I had was that Spider Sabich also failed to qualify. At least I wasn't going to be overtaken for the lead because of my poor showing.

When you stop to think of it, it was a kind of anomalous situation. The two top drawing cards, battling for the overall lead, both failed to qualify. The ISRA people were not very pleased by this. And quite frankly, I felt the system wasn't very good if it allowed the crowd to be disappointed this way. My view is that there should be an automatic qualification for the top skiers on the money list. The top four, let's say. That way, the drama of the battle for the lead would continue into the man-to-man races, at least for one round, and the spectators wouldn't feel gypped.

In Park City, the problem wasn't as bad as it might be, say, in Boyne. Park City is only a thirty-minute drive from Salt Lake. But Boyne is a long drive from Detroit or Chicago. If a guy drives five or six hours to watch Sabich and Killy racing, he's going to feel cheated if he gets there to find that neither one will be racing that day. If the word gets around that it's always a gamble whether or not you'll get to see your favorite, it will hurt attendance. ISRA ought to change this rule to provide automatic qualification of the top racers on the money list. I think that would be an improvement in the format.

With both Spider and me out of the race, the way was open for Stuefer to make the most of the opportunity. And it looked as though that's just what he was going to do. In the opening round, he beat Duncan Cullman, an American independent who had the reputation of being some kind of oddball. His sponsor's bib carried the name "St. Bernard Monastery," and there were stories that Cullman was busy writing poetry in between races. He was unlucky against Stuefer, though, because he fell badly and tore some ligaments in his knee, putting him on crutches for several days.

Next, Stuefer faced Dan Mooney, but this wasn't Mooney's day. And in the semifinals, Stuefer beat Terje Overland. His opponent in the finals was his countryman Hugo Nindl. They were running the course neck and neck until about halfway down, when Nindl lost his balance between the second and third jumps and almost fell. Stuefer shot out ahead and took the run by 1.358 seconds—an enormous margin which just about sewed up the victory for Stuefer.

But Nindl is not one who gives up easily. He was slightly ahead as the two racers came into the second bump when suddenly Stuefer fell. He had made a mistake in the gate just before the jump and couldn't correct in time—and that was it. Despite an almost insurmountable lead in the first run, he lost to Nindl. That left him still eight points behind me in the overall standings.

As I wasn't racing, I busied myself taking pictures. Photographer John Russell loaned me a camera and I posted myself on the course just below the second bump. I knew just how the racers would hit the bump so I was able to figure out what the most dramatic moment would be to click the shutter. Sure enough, Russell confessed to me afterward that my shots were the best he had of that race.

On Sunday, it was dark with snow clouds, and it was soon apparent the race could not be held. It was windy and snowing heavily. Never before in ISRA history had a race been postponed, but the officials, after inspecting the course (actually, they had trouble finding it), looking at the sky, and consulting the meteorologists, decided there was always a first time. A good thing, too, since over a foot of snow fell on Sunday.

Monday didn't look much more promising. But the snow did stop for a while, so it was decided to hold the slalom. Then all kinds of problems began to develop. A timing light blew out, so they postponed the qualification round. There was a rock in the middle of the first jump, so the course had to be reset. Then one of the electronic starters fell in the snow, causing a malfunction and another delay. Normally, we start the qualifications around 10 A.M. This day, they began around noon.

There were forty gates on this course, and after all that fresh snow, we had to contend with ruts as deep as irrigation ditches. After the first run of the qualifications, it was unbelievable. Not only didn't I qualify, but neither did Sabich, Stuefer, or Nindl. The four top racers in the season's standings, and not a one of us qualified on the first run. Fortunately, on our second runs, we all managed to squeak by. But the possibility that none of us might have made it into the race underscored the soundness of my view that the top contenders should qualify automatically.

Even though it was a Monday and the weather was threatening, a fairly good crowd turned out—something like 3,000 spectators. In this treacherous snow, they saw some spectacular falls. After the opening round, where I skied quite well, I regained my confidence. In the quarterfinals, I faced Lasse Hamre, and in the first run I took a 1.32-second lead—big enough to relax on my second run. But then, just a couple of gates out of the start, I caught an outside edge. That was the first time in my life I had ever done that. I fell and was out of the race.

Catching an outside edge—for me, that was unbelievable. The bottom of an Alpine ski has a metal edge on each side running from tip to tail. When you stand on your skis, the edges of the two skis that are nearest each other are called the inside edges; the ones on the exterior sides away from each other are the outside edges. When racers turn their skis, they usually carve into the snow with the metal edges of the skis.

To *catch* an edge is to carve into the snow when you want the ski to slide over the snow. It is fairly commonplace to catch an inside edge, that is, inadvertently to roll your feet inward so that your skis get on one or the other of the inside edges when you want them to stay flat. But even if you try to do it, it is very hard to catch an outside edge. Yet, whether from fatigue or failure to concentrate, that's what I did.

Sabich and Stuefer were now both in a position to take over the lead in the money list. Sabich looked like he was trying too hard in the quarterfinals when he went against Norbert Wender, an Austrian racing for Atomic Skis. Near the top of the first run, Sabich fell. But he refused to give up, and scampered back onto his skis to continue down the course, even though he was now trailing by three gates. This refusal to admit defeat paid off. Apparently Wender was unaware Sabich had fallen, and he continued to ski aggressively. Unfortunately, he hit a rut and blew off the course, giving the match to Spider. Against Hamre in the semifinals, though, Spider got in trouble, started forcing to pick up the time he had lost, and ended up skiing off the course about halfway down.

As for Stuefer, he beat Overland in the quarterfinals. In the semifinals, Stuefer faced Nindl again, but ran into some ruts and lost time. So Nindl faced Hamre for the finals, took a .493-of-a-second lead in the first run, and won when Hamre skied off the course in the second run.

In the consolation round, Stuefer took third and Sabich fourth. That meant that Stuefer was now tied with me for first in the overall standings, with Sabich only two points behind us. Nindl, the only racer that season to have won back-to-back victories in giant slalom and slalom, was fourth and had enough points to have an outside chance of winning. Tschudi, Penz, Milne, and Mooney from Team Rossignol were all in the first ten, but after Nindl, no one was given much chance of catching up with the leaders.

Though Nindl was the only one to come up with a double victory at any race up to that point in the season, he was quite frank in admitting he couldn't have done it under normal circumstances. Said Hugo, "I wouldn't have been able to make it if Sunday's race hadn't been canceled. I was too tired yesterday. I needed that day's rest."

There was a two-week break between the Park City race and the next-to-last event, which was coming up at Steamboat, Colorado. It was a busy period for me. I flew to Denver and then drove to Breckenridge where I met Al Greenberg, editor of *Skiing Magazine,* to tape a series of articles I was doing for the following season's magazines. And there was also some promotional work I had to do to fulfill my obligations to Breckenridge. Finally, I was to give some ski lessons to Lynn Thornberry, a writer from *Ladies' Home Journal* who had never been on skis before. She was doing a story about how I taught her to ski.

Except for my adventure with the Argentine army, I had never before tried to teach a beginner to ski. One should really start out on flat land, walk around and get the feel of the skis, learn how to sidestep, herringbone, do kickturns, fall down and get up, and a lot of such maneuvers before one takes a lift up the mountain.

But that isn't very glamorous, and I wanted her to have a good article. So I thought I could take her up on the chair lift and come down a gentle slope. First I taught her to sideslip and then to snowplow, but she really didn't know how to control her skis. And suddenly, she caught an edge and started to ski straight down the hill. There were people all over the slope and trees to either side, and there she was, out of control, picking up speed at an alarming rate, and there was nothing I could do for her.

I was quite frightened, skiing alongside her trying to get her to put her skis back in a snowplow position and slow down by applying pressure to her inside edges. But she was too frightened herself to do anything except head straight downhill. Finally, all I could think of was to pick her up in my arms, make a long turn and come to a stop and put her down again. She was obviously upset, but she didn't say anything, and neither did I.

Teaching beginning skiers is a *métier* in itself. It may have been a good story idea to go to the world's leading ski racer for lessons, but I'm afraid Jean-Claude Killy is not the world's leading ski instructor. Ms. Thornberry would have been better off learning from a good teacher who has studied the techniques of introducing a beginner to the sport. For me it was a lesson in how difficult it is to teach someone else the movements that are second nature to me.

At the end of the week, I skied at Copper Mountain, a new Colorado area not far from Breckenridge, where we were joined by photographer John Russell and Michel's wife Chantal. We had some discussions with Gary Mitchell of the Copper Mountain management about the possibility of using Copper as home base for the Rossignol team. In the evening, we ate a great fish dinner at John Russell's house. John had been taking a lot of pictures of me on the tour—among them, the photos illustrating this text.

Next day, we had to be in Las Vegas—not for amusement,

but to work. Each spring, the manufacturers and distributors of ski apparel and equipment have a marketing show where they exhibit their lines for the following season to ski shop owners and buyers. The manufacturers and distributors belong to an organization called Ski Industries America, and the only way to sell ski-related merchandise in the United States is to be at these shows. The reason this show, like so many like it, is held in Las Vegas is that exhibit space in the Las Vegas Convention Hall is large enough and inexpensive enough to attract the manufacturers. The gambling casinos and big-name entertainment help increase attendance at these shows, so the exhibitors keep coming back.

I was expected to spend a certain amount of time at the Rossignol booth talking with retailers about Rossignol skis. This was also an opportunity for me to talk with ski-industry people about various contracts I was involved in—or to discuss the possibility of new ones. As for playing—I played a lot of golf at Las Vegas, but I'm not really one for spending much time at the gaming tables. It's funny, I used to gamble a lot when I couldn't afford to lose. Now that I can, it's no longer as exciting for me, so I rarely do it.

I did play blackjack one night. I had seen a pair of golf shoes that day; they cost $40 and I couldn't decide whether to buy them. But that night, I decided I would play some blackjack to see if I could win enough to buy the shoes. We were staying at the Stardust, so I headed down to the tables early in the evening to play until we were ready to go to dinner. And I got lucky. I just sat there for a short time—maybe a half hour—and I won $200. But the next day, I found they didn't have those golf shoes in my size. Michel, who knew my plan to win enough to get those shoes, asked me what happened, and I told him, "I couldn't find any $200 golf shoes."

Las Vegas is a strange place—mountains all around, but totally unrelated to the town, which looks like it was set down in the desert by a bunch of electrical sign companies looking for a place to test their wares. I know of no sadder sight than the blank looks on the faces of the seedy characters who stand in front of the slot machines for hours on end dropping coins into these mechanical monsters. But the entertainment there is really tops. We went to the Bill Cosby show at the Hilton and found it first rate.

Las Vegas aside, I love the ski shows. It's a chance for me to see all my old friends—racers, manufacturers, and others associated with the ski business. I ran into Michel Hofstetter of Hofstetter Sports, the largest ski store in Geneva, and got news from home. And of course, there was the whole Rossignol and Trappeur group, with whom we could discuss equipment questions and plans for the following season. There are shows like this in Europe, too—in Grenoble, France, and Munich, Germany. Many of the people at Las Vegas go to all the major shows of this nature, so they know all the gossip there is to know about the ski world. I'd hate to have to make the whole tour, but I never let a year go by without dropping in on at least one of these shows.

On Tuesday, we flew to Denver and rented cars for the trip to Steamboat Springs. For many years on the amateur circuit, I used to see on the lists of skiers and where they came from frequent mention of the town of Steamboat Springs, Colorado. More members of U.S. Olympic ski teams have come from Steamboat Springs than from any other town in the U.S. I always wondered what kind of place it was. I figured, if it produced all those good racers, it must be a big ski resort like Chamonix or Megève.

This was the first time I had a chance to visit the town, and it wasn't at all what I expected—just a small little Western cow town. Not even a mountain town, really. There are mountains all around, but the town is in a valley, and what mountains you can see look kind of tame. It was hard to imagine such a town producing the Werners (Bud, Skeeter, and Loris), Moose Barrows (his crash in the downhill at Grenoble was probably the most photographed fall that skiing has ever produced), Jere Elliot, Gordy Wren, Marv Crawford, and other top U.S. competitors. But Bud Werner, until he was killed in an avalanche in 1964, was generally regarded as the finest skier the United States had ever produced. The mountain at Steamboat Springs is called Mt. Werner in his honor.

What the town always had, I understand, was a lot of spirit, but this isn't evident to the eye of the casual visitor. The name Steamboat Springs came from some hot underground springs that used to make a noise like a steamboat whistle, or so legend has it. There are still plenty of hot springs around Steamboat, and some of them even make noise. Skiers sometimes go out and bathe in them—but you have to be careful. They can be scalding hot, and if you don't know which ones are safe, it's best not to risk the dip.

The ski area is fairly impressive, though I understand this is all of very recent date. A big corporation bought the resort a few years ago and started investing heavily in lifts and in a vacation village at the base of the mountain. This is only about a mile or so out of town. The area where the Werners, Moose Barrows, and the others got their start, though, was at a much smaller place on the opposite end of town—really right inside the village. This is called Howelsen Hill, and apparently, the reason Steamboat produced so many good racers is that the kids would go there every day right after school to jump and run gates.

That's all it takes to produce racers—a program that will get young kids to run through slalom gates every day. The United States has mountains that are big enough, snow that is deep enough, and kids who want to try hard enough. There really is no reason why U.S. racers can't rank with the best. Steamboat Springs proves that. If it was so successful in earlier years, now that it had a major resort developed on a really big mountain, it ought to produce many more outstanding racers.

Tom Krebsbach, my friend from Minnesota, owns a condominium at Steamboat, and he put us up at his place, once again overwhelming us with his gracious hospitality. The entire stay was a delight not only because of Tom, but because that old Colorado magic was at work again: sun, blue sky, fluffy light snow. I did a lot of free skiing the first day or two, just enjoying the mountain. There's a long gondola that takes you up to what had appeared from below to be the summit. Once on top, though, you realize this is only halfway up. There's a complex of chair lifts, each one going up to what you think is the summit, only to see another chunk of mountain beyond. At the very top is an automatic Poma—a very common sight in France, but this was the first I had seen in this country—taking you up a treeless slope to a marvelous panorama of Rocky peaks in the distance.

The treeless mountaintops in Colorado, by the way, are not the result of being above the timber line, as in the Alps. Here, the story goes, these mountaintops were set ablaze by the Indians in the late nineteenth century as a form of protest against the invasion of the white man. If the story is true, the protest was quite ineffectual; today, skiers can only be grateful that it has left a legacy of marvelous bowls and open slope skiing. Still, it's a pity that all that spruce and fir and aspen is gone forever.

Michel was still working on my boots, and he also had me try a new pair of giant slalom skis—my sixth pair. Again, these were Roc 550s, and they were very good. I liked my new boots, too. Michel worked them over by putting more material into the right boot so it held my foot better. Later on, while skiing, it began to hurt, so right out there on the snow he cut the inner boot to reduce the friction.

There was a pro–am race here, too, and some of the same celebrities who had been at Bear Valley showed up to compete—including Mrs. Kennedy. In this case, she did insist on being teamed with me—she made it a condition of her appearing, I understand. Here, however, the rules were different; there were three to a team instead of two. On the team with Mrs. Kennedy and myself was Ronnie Connelly, a local ski school instructor, so it looked like quite a formidable team.

Clint Eastwood, who couldn't seem to get enough of this kind of competition, was there, too, and he was teamed with Jake Hoeschler and Jake's wife Janice. Hoeschler showed up at every race on the circuit and ran in every qualifying elimination only to have the unique distinction of having failed to qualify in every race during that season. Though Clint Eastwood was as full of determination as ever, his technique hadn't advanced much from Bear Valley, so his team was not very formidable looking.

More of a threat was the team of Spider Sabich, Claudine Longet, and Dick Anderson (the Miami Dolphins football player).

In the race, Mrs. Kennedy was as aggressive as ever—perhaps a little too much. She fell and was out of contention. She insisted on getting up again and finishing, however—quite in keeping with her character. But her time was seventieth out of the seventy-five finishers. At least she was not among the eighteen DNF (Did Not Finish) skiers.

Even if Mrs. Kennedy had not fallen, our team might not have won, since my time was only second best overall. Duncan Cullman had an excellent run and his team won, although it hardly qualified as celebrity or amateur, since the other two team members were Chuck Stoughton, a Steamboat realtor who skied regularly, and Dick Randolph, the area's assistant general manager.

In second place in the event was the team of Moose Barrows, Doak Walker, and Gretchen Raubfogel.

That was a popular result, since Moose was a native of Steamboat and Doak Walker, a former professional football player, was married to Skeeter Werner, a former member of the U.S. Olympic Team herself and the owner of a couple of ski shops in Steamboat. Gretchen Raubfogel was the Snow Queen of Frontier Airlines, which served Steamboat.

The Killy–Kennedy–Connelly team finished twenty-fourth out of thirty-one.

Among the spectators at Steamboat was Mark McCormack. He had never seen a pro race before and wanted to come size up for himself what the potential might be, to see whether he agreed it was worth it for me to invest so much time and effort—and if so, to see what would be required of his organization to do a better job for me.

His reaction was exactly what I had expected—full of enthusiasm. He hadn't expected to see such excitement, to see such a big crowd or such a vociferous crowd. The competition was of a higher level than he had imagined it to be, the courses more difficult, and the format easier to grasp for the nonskier. I was glad he had made the trip over so that he could understand first-hand what this tour was all about.

For the giant slalom on Saturday, the snow was iced over somewhat, the light was flat, and it was snowing, though not heavily. The course had been prepared by Bud Werner's brother Loris, who ran the ski school here, and it was a beautiful job. There were twenty-two gates to the course, with the biggest bumps we had seen all year. The first one was well over eight feet high.

I was racing very well. I had the best qualifying time and easily took Terje Overland in the opening round. Then, in the quarter-finals against Tschudi, I ran into equipment difficulties. Coming off that big first jump, I landed so hard, I broke my left ski. Fortunately, it didn't throw me, and I was still able to win that run.

Michel came rushing up with another pair of skis, but I told him I would change only the left ski, the broken one, and keep my good right ski.

"That's crazy," he said. "You won't have a pair. They won't react in the same way and you won't be able to ski as well."

"Look, Michel," I said. "We haven't tested this new pair. For all we know, it might be a second or two slower. If this pair isn't as good and I change only one ski, I'll be penalized only half as much. Less, in fact, because I can always rely more on my right ski, on the one I know is good.

Michel was reluctant to do this. It violated all his theories about the need for meticulous care in matching a pair of skis. But he finally let me do as I wanted—and I won. I then beat Hans Bjorge in the semifinals and faced Dan Mooney in the finals. Mooney was also skiing extremely well that day, and I edged him by only .368 of a second in the first run. In the second run, Mooney had trouble off that big bump and skied off the course.

My victory, my sixth of the season, put me back in first place, eighteen points ahead of Stuefer and twenty ahead of Sabich. But in taking one of the gates close, I rammed my hand against the pole, and so unyielding were these poles that I badly hurt my knuckles. I was unable to shake hands with any of my well-wishers. I was also afraid I would have trouble holding my pole the next day. Now with both my knee and my knuckles in bandages, I was relieved that this was the next to last stop of the season.

Sunday was one of those classic Colorado days. More snow had fallen, the sun was out, the sky was clear, and a good crowd was on hand to watch. I was feeling strong enough to win this time, and I felt I was skiing well enough to make this the breakthrough. A first would not mathematically eliminate either Sabich or Stuefer, but it would make it all but impossible for them to overtake me.

My spirits went up when I had the best qualifying time on my course—and Harald Stuefer, who had come to Steamboat tied with me for first and was the only man on the circuit who had never missed qualifying this season—finally missed.

I started the slalom well, beating Sturm in the opening round and Perry Thompson in the quarterfinals. And whom should I face in the semifinals but Alain Penz! Barring a foolish error, I knew I could beat Alain. So I skied very cautiously in the upper part of the course, which was particularly difficult, and took the first run by .170 of a second—a small margin to be sure. In the second run, I again was cautious up on top, but then in the flat part near the finish, just before the last jump, I made an error. I took one gate too wide so that I lost speed in a section where I couldn't get it back. Alain, meantime, took every risk he could and made it across the finish .202 of a second ahead of me—which meant his combined time was .032 of a second faster for the two runs.

When I called Danièle that night to tell her what had happened, she was just furious at this result. "Alain has no chance to win the World Cup," she said. She always called the Benson & Hedges Grand Prix the World Cup. "He should have let you win."

"Let me win? Why should he do that? Even if we were close friends, he'd be hurting himself. He has a chance to get some of the Grand Prix money even if he can't win first prize anymore. He'd be foolish to sacrifice his own chances."

"Rossignol should pay him to let you win," she said. "Just like they do in bike racing. The guy who has the best chance always has the rest of the team riding in front of him to make things easier so he doesn't get too tired to beat the top man of the other teams."

I tried to explain to her that bike racing and ski racing are two different things. In a bicycle race, if you follow another racer, allowing him to break the air, you do much less work. In a bike pack, the lead constantly changes to avoid tiring anyone too much. But the guy you figure has the best chance on your team to win will be allowed to skip his turn at the head of the pack, always pedaling in second spot where it's like pedaling in a vacuum. In professional bike racing, this is organized to the point where everyone knows that some racers will pay the other team members to run interference for them.

But this couldn't work in ski racing. As I pointed out to Danièle, Penz's contract with Rossignol depends on how well he does. They can't offer him money to lose to me and then later say they won't pay him more for next year because he didn't win enough. It's in his interest to win as much as he can, not just for the prize money, but to improve his bargaining position. If he can't get what he wants from Rossignol, he can go to another manufacturer and point to his record. It wouldn't be too impressive if he had to say "In such-and-such a race, I threw it so Jean-Claude could win." If that company went and checked with Rossignol, they would have to deny it. If the story got out, it would be a *scandale* that would not only hurt me, but would be bad for Rossignol, too. It would kill the sport.

Despite my argument, I'm afraid Danièle couldn't appreciate the difference between an individual sport like skiing and a sport like cycling where team effort was involved even if the ultimate victory belonged to the individual. But she did change her tune when I suggested she think of it with the shoe on the other foot:

"Suppose Penz were in contention and I had no chance of winning. It could well have taken me more than one season to get back into winning form. Or I could have had an injury midseason. In such a situation, would you want Rossignol to pay me to deliberately let Penz win?"

She had no answer to that. But she was still furious that Penz had beaten me. That upset her more than when any other racer had turned the trick.

With all that, the weekend's results weren't too bad for me. I had my sixth giant slalom win of the year. And after Penz beat me in the slalom semifinals, I went on to face Doug Woodcock in the consolation round and ended in third place when Woodcock disqualified. That boosted my point total for the season to 288 and my winnings to $25,900. I was now thirty points ahead of Sabich and thirty-three points ahead of Stuefer. No one else had a mathematical chance of overtaking me. Theoretically, I could still blow it. If I failed to qualify in both of the next races and Stuefer and Sabich shared firsts and seconds, I could even end up in third. But that was unlikely. I now had a substantial lead, and with the last races of the season only two weeks off, I was feeling pretty confident.

Then it was back to Breckenridge to shoot the Goodyear commercial. I had to get up at five every morning. While the snow was still firm, we would pull a car up behind a snowcat. The car was outfitted with Goodyear's Winterguard radial snow tires, and I would drive the car down through the slalom course. Then I would ski through the same gates. The idea was to show these two actions on a split screen to prove that these tires track as well as a pair of slalom skis. Actually, the car held the course surprisingly well.

But this was long hard work. They started filming at six, and after the sun had warmed up the slopes so we couldn't use the course any more, we would do other shots for the commercial, working till four or five in the afternoon. I had a congested throat, so I found this work, which went on for three days, extremely exhausting.

Meantime, Michel continued to work on my equipment, in particular on my boots. He tried injecting different polyurethane or silicone foams into my Trappeur shells. At Jean-Paul Jallifier's shop in Aspen, he even tried the Lange foam. As the upcoming race at Aspen Highlands was called the Lange Cup, it would have been appropriate if I ended up using something from the

Lange Company, the sponsors. But I finally went back to the regular Trappeur foam as best for my feet.

The stage was set for the payoff. I had begun the season ignominiously at Aspen. I now hoped to finish it there—in a blaze of glory.

12
PULL IT OFF

ASPEN is the town most Europeans think of first when one mentions American skiing. Sun Valley's ski runs were developed first. Jackson Hole's mountain is bigger. Heavenly Valley's nightlife is livelier. Alta's snow is more powdery. But nowhere in the United States is there a combination of attributes to equal Aspen's.

Aspen, like Park City, Breckenridge, and Telluride, is a former mining town. Unlike Sun Valley, Snowmass, Vail, and most of the modern European ski resorts, Aspen has a history, an existence apart from its skiing. It is authentically American, which is not the case for many of the U.S. areas I visited which seemed like imitations of Swiss or Tyrolean villages—in most cases, poor imitations. Aspen couldn't be anywhere else but in the United States, with its old two- and three-story Victorian houses, its corner drug stores, steak houses, supermarkets, silversmiths, and the other vestiges of its heyday as a nineteenth century boom town when silver mining was at its peak.

Aspen is a many-faceted place. It's a center for ski bums, for young people not particularly dedicated to skiing but who like the free and easy atmosphere of a resort town where the turned-on kids come to ski. Aspen is also a tourist town that attracts well-to-do people who like to ski, to eat in fine restaurants like The Copper Kettle, and to listen to the live combos in the jammed night spots around town. The underground Aspen attracts college dropouts, kids into dope and stronger drugs—and those who just want to be where the good skiing is.

The town is laid out in squares, snuggled right up against Ajax Mountain (that's what they now call Aspen Mountain). The lifts on Ajax belong to the Aspen Skiing Corp. Just out of town, there is Buttermilk, a large, gentle mountain used mostly for teaching beginners and low intermediates. This, too, belongs to the Aspen Skiing Corp. (almost universally called simply, the Ski Corp.). Still a third resort where the lifts are run by the Ski Corp. is Snowmass, about eight miles out of town.

Finally, between Ajax and Buttermilk there is one more area, this one called Aspen Highlands. It is *not* owned by the Ski Corp. but by a man named Whip Jones. In fact, there is a good deal of rivalry between the two.

It was at Aspen Highlands that the last race of the ISRA tour was to be held.

Naturally, I went into this race a heavy favorite. With a lead of thirty points, it was only natural that I should be the favorite. But I can't in all honesty say that I was the favorite of the Aspen locals who came out to watch. There were several reasons for this.

During most of the tour, it was obvious that the crowds were rooting for me. Mostly, I suppose, this was because I was the best known. And as I've mentioned, I think the crowd was impressed that I was offering these young unknown skiers the chance to beat the great Killy. The spectators could sense that every racer who faced me was putting out something extra, not just to win a race, but to win this private race against Killy.

Beating Spider Sabich, for example, didn't carry the same prestige. Spider was the reigning pro champ, but he hadn't won everything there was to win in the world of skiing as I had. If a racer could beat me, it almost didn't matter whether he went on to win or not. He still could say he had beaten Killy.

Of course, that worked two ways. Though my opponents would be trying harder just because they were paired with me, they were also more nervous and, because they were pressing harder, more apt to make a mistake. Still, I'm sure part of the reason the crowds were so enthusiastically behind me was this knowledge that I was holding myself up as a target, allowing the whole field to take shots at me.

In Aspen, though, things were different. I had my supporters, of course. Plenty of them. But the typical young hot-dog skier was not in my camp. I was too straight for them. Their favorites were what they called "the turned-on skiers." There were several racers on the pro circuit who seemed to be on some constant high. In a few cases, I'm certain they were taking or smoking some kind of drugs. In other cases, they may just have acted doped up, but the effect on the Aspen underground culture was the same. It almost seemed that the wackier the behavior, the louder the cheering section.

There was another aspect to crowd attitudes—and to the determination of some of the competitors. Though the overall ISRA tour was sponsored by the Benson & Hedges cigarette people, each individual race also had other sponsors. In one case, it was Samsonite Luggage; in another, United Air Lines; or still another, MacDonald's Hamburgers; or again, Miller's Beer. Sometimes, though, the sponsor was a ski equipment manufacturer. At Boyne, for example, the race was for the K2 Cup.

Not surprisingly, at Boyne there was a strong rooting section —made up of K2 personnel who were on the scene in force— voicing support for K2s skiers: Spider Sabich, Rudd Pyles, and Peter Duncan. Not that it did them much good. As you may remember, at Boyne, I beat Spider in the giant slalom finals and then took third in the slalom while Spider watched, having failed to qualify in that race.

At Aspen, this company-support phenomenon was even more marked. This last race was sponsored by Lange Boots—it was the fourth annual Lange Cup race. And since the Lange factory is in Bloomfield, Colorado, a strong Lange rooting section was on hand to cheer the Lange team racer, Tyler Palmer.

Among the other pros, there's little doubt I was not the favorite. Some felt it wasn't good for the reputation of the circuit for me to come out of retirement and win, even if I hadn't exactly walked all over everyone. There was also some resentment at the ease with which the Rossignol juggernaut—as it had come to be called—had dominated the team standings. And I was blamed for that.

Perhaps there was an element of anti-French feeling, too. There were a lot of Austrians on the circuit, and their favorite was probably Harald Stuefer, who was generally popular because he never said very much and was therefore noncontroversial. Spider was also favored by many because he was a mixer, one of the boys. And he was respected because he had worked hard to make pro racing big.

I think all the racers recognized that my presence on the circuit had been good for attendance and press coverage—and therefore good for everyone. Nevertheless, for a variety of reasons, I think most of the other pros would have been just as happy to see me come to grief at Aspen.

Not that any of this bothered me. The figures really favored me. Even if I did no better than fourth each day, Spider would have to put back-to-back victories together just to tie me. If I won the giant slalom, as I had been doing pretty regularly, it was all over. The Grand Prix would be mine.

Instead of running the races on Saturday and Sunday, as had been the custom up to this point, Aspen Highlands decided to run the giant slalom on Friday and the slalom on Saturday, perhaps so as not to interfere too much with weekend recreational skiers. For this late in the season—a season that had not been especially ample in snow cover—the conditions at Aspen Highlands were remarkably good. The highest point served by the area's lifts—Loges Peak—is around 12,000 feet above sea level, so there was no fear that the races couldn't be held in April. But it was thought probable that the courses would have to be laid out above the midstation.

Instead, the snow was good at the base, 3,800 feet below the top of Loges Peak, which meant the crowds would have easy access to the course. And the crowds were good; the estimate was that there were close to 5,000 for the final event.

Friday, it was warm and sunshiny. The course was the longest of the year, and despite the high temperatures, probably the fastest. It had thirty-one gates, and it made a long, gentle bend, though there were not really any sharp giant slalom-type turns. It was deceptively fast, particularly off the bumps. At first, the racers criticized it because they thought it was too easy. Then they criticized it because they thought it was too fast and tricky.

What really upset them is that the course had been set by Michel Arpin.

The critics were saying that Michel had set a course that would be specially suited to my style. And they said that he would be able to warn me of any places that might present problems. Now, as a matter of fact, Michel has learned not to warn me of any particularly troublesome spot on a course. Inevitably when he does, that's exactly where I have problems. If I look the course over and see the same spot myself, I'll do all right. Michel thinks there must be something psychological about this, but I'm not sure what's involved.

Anyway, it's absurd to think that I would do best on a course without any giant slalom type turns. When I was an amateur, though I dominated all three events, giant slalom was always considered my best event. As a pro, so far, I had won six giant slaloms during the season. A giant slalom course that was non-GS-y—atypical—was hardly one designed specially for me.

But nobody believed that. There were comments that too much was at stake here, and that a neutral party should have been named to set the course. Perhaps so. But we hadn't asked for this. Moose Barrows, the racers' representative within ISRA, came to Michel and asked him to set it up. It was not unusual to ask a technician like Michel to do this, but this was the first time during the season they had come to him. The criticism, I think, was just an indication of how tense everyone was for this final event.

This backbiting talk continued until the opening round. I had had a good qualification, was confident that my equipment was right, and on Friday, started out skiing very well, obviously off to an excellent day. I was matched against Otto Tschudi, one of my teammates from Rossignol, who was in contention for fifth place overall. I knew Otto was suffering from a fever and was not at his best, but in this last event of the season, you could never tell. A lot was at stake for both of us.

I zipped through the course, but on the last bump, I blasted off going too fast and with a bad line. I couldn't correct mid-air, and I just shot right off the course. I was leading Tschudi by almost a full gate at that point, and what was even more bizarre, he had fallen at almost the same moment I had. But I was off the course, so even without finishing the race, he moved into the quarterfinals. In effect, the tricky course Michel had set claimed me as one of its first victims.

This was what Sabich and Stuefer were waiting for. I had added only five points to my total by qualifying. Nobody considered me much of a threat in slalom—at any rate, I hadn't been able to win one all season. If Spider could win the giant slalom, he'd be only ten points behind going into the slalom, giving him a good chance to overtake me. It was basically the same story for Stuefer, except he was an additional three points behind.

So I spent the rest of the day watching to see how my two rivals would make out. Danièle had returned from Geneva to be with me in what we had both assumed would be my hour of victory, and her tenseness over the situation began to affect my nerves. My father had also come over from Val d'Isère, and I was hoping his trip wasn't going to be a disappointment, that he wasn't going to be here just to commiserate with me.

Stuefer faced Rudd Pyles in the opening round and took his measure. Duncan Cullman, who was back on his skis after his knee injury, was his next victim. In the semifinals, he beat Hans Bjorge. It looked good for Stuefer.

Spider was also making the most of the opportunity. He beat René Techer in the opening round although he had some difficulty coming off a couple of the bumps. Then he took Malcolm Milne in the quarterfinals, and met Hugo Nindl in the semifinals.

Hugo still had a chance for third place, and he wasn't about to give up. He was skiing extremely well, and by the time they came to the second bump, Sabich was behind. He was pushing to catch up and moving pretty fast—probably going over fifty miles an hour at that point. At the top of the bump, his arm caught on the gate and just flipped him over like a twirling baton. He landed right on the back of his neck—and it was obvious he was hurt badly. He was rushed to the hospital.

Spider and I had not become very close over the season. Though Claudine Longet, his girl friend, and Danièle were good friends, we didn't socialize much as couples. The fault was certainly not Spider's; he would have liked me to mix more with the other racers. But the ways of other racers are not my ways, and I'm afraid I always maintained a certain distance. Though this was often misinterpreted as snobbism or even dislike, that was certainly not the case.

At any rate, I was terribly distressed to see Spider get hurt. I don't think he was skiing as well as I had seen him ski at other times during the season, so there was no question about being relieved I wouldn't be facing him the next day. I think I could have beaten him—even at his best—and it would have added to the drama if he had been racing. In any event, no one likes to win through another's injury.

Fortunately, it turned out Spider had not been seriously hurt. He was diagnosed in the Aspen Hospital as having a compression fracture of the eighth vertebra and a sprained ankle. He was back as a spectator the next day, wearing a back brace.

With Spider out, all the drama now centered on the final between Harald Stuefer and Hugo Nindl. I was rooting for Hugo, of course. Even if it would not have been to my advantage to have him beat Stuefer, I would have been for him just because I liked him. That he was an Austrian made no difference to me. I admired his courage—he had broken both his legs as an amateur, thus ending his racing career when he might easily have become the world's best. After a long recovery, he became a ski instructor, and then was one of the earliest ones on the pro racing circuit. As I've mentioned, I found him and other older racers more *sympa,* easier for me to relate to.

In the first run, Hugo shot out of the gate first and briefly held the lead; but Stuefer overtook him to win by .376 of a second. Hugo looked a little tired, but in the second run, he again shot out in front, only to be overtaken once again, this time losing by .512 of a second. Stuefer was hot on my trail.

Friday night, a heavy snowstorm moved in, and for the slalom on Saturday, it was almost a complete whiteout. Both Stuefer and I managed to qualify. Nindl, who would have passed Sabich for third if he had done well in slalom, was just too tired and failed to make the cut. The best qualifying time of the day went to Hank Kashiwa, showing once again that he really has the potential people see in him. What he lacks is consistency. Later, he was disqualified in the opening round.

Because of the weather, there was a big confab over whether to postpone the slalom races till Sunday. I was all for going ahead. I had had only two runs the day before, so I was fresh and ready to go. Stuefer had run the course nine times and had to be feeling the effects. But the race officials were concerned that the crowd would be small and wouldn't be able to see their favorites. They decided to postpone.

Karl Schranz and Werner Bleiner, the former Austrian team members had come to Aspen to watch the races. It was expected that they would join the circuit for 1973–74 and they wanted to look things over before making up their minds. I had dinner that night with Karl—the first time this had happened, though we had known each other ever since I first began winning on the international circuit. We were always rivals and very different sorts of personalities. He was frequently abrupt with the press and had the image of a kind of bad guy, a prima donna who wasn't even liked by the Austrian team members. I think Karl rather enjoyed this bad-guy image. He was really very dedicated to the sport and not a difficult person to get along with when you got to know him.

"I probably would have been your friend if you hadn't been Austrian," I told him. He made no response to this, sticking to the business at hand—which was, for him, to find out everything he could about the pro circuit.

From the race organizers' point of view, the slalom postponement turned out to be a good decision. On Sunday, the skies were clear again, three parachutists dropped onto the slopes to start things off, a large crowd was on hand, and all the pomp and ceremony Aspen Highlands could muster was put on display. Not that any extra excitement was needed. The race had plenty of its own.

Stuefer was now only thirteen points behind me. If he won the slalom, I would have to do no worse than third to hold my lead. The word was out that a lot of betting was going against me. I guess that made sense.

First of all, I hadn't won a slalom all season. And I had never had a better finish in slalom than I had had in giant slalom. But the main reason I was the underdog was the course. Set by Jamie Corriveau of K2, it had fifty-one gates, by far the longest we had raced all season. What's more, the gates were tightly set. Everyone was sure that I didn't have the strength to run a course like this and win. Nobody said that Corriveau may have deliberately set the course so it would be tough for me. After all, with Spider out of the running, Corriveau would appear to be neutral, right?

Not every bettor was putting his money on Stuefer, though. As I stood in the starting gate for my first run, one spectator yelled encouragement to me, adding, "Ya gotta do well, Killy. I got five dollars bet on you."

I turned to this big sport, smiled, and said, "Oh, the pressure." One of the newsmen there later picked this up and used it in the headline for his story.

In the opening round, I faced Roland Gay. He was trying too hard and disqualified. Meanwhile, Harald Stuefer was facing Doug Woodcock, who also disqualified.

My next opponent was Alain Penz. I remembered Danièle's feelings about Penz's victory over me at Steamboat. How would I feel now if I knew Penz was going to let me win instead of trying his best to beat me? It was a tempting thought, but I knew Penz would never do it even if I would have sanctioned it. He was still in contention with Tschudi for fifth place money. Penz, now that he had the confidence of having conquered me once, was going to be hard to beat, no doubt about that.

Out of the starting gate we went, and I could hear Penz's skis alongside me. Then he started to gain and at one point was nearly two gates ahead. Going into the last bump, I could see he was still slightly ahead, and try as I could, I wasn't able to overtake him.

Tyler Palmer was Harald Stuefer's opponent in the quarter-finals, and Palmer also took the first run—by .183 of a second. Stuefer had come back from lots worse handicaps than that, so I knew it was up to me to make my second run against Penz a good one.

And it was. I got out of the gate fast, got a good rhythm going, and despite the length of the course, kept up my speed all the way. Penz's margin in the first run had been .223 of a second. In the second run, I went through the finish line .875 of a second ahead of him for a combined margin of .652 of a second.

At that point, I thought Stuefer could still win. If he took first and I lost in both the semifinals and the consolation round, he would win by two points. It wasn't over yet.

But suddenly, it was. Tyler Palmer, with the whole Lange factory there to cheer him on, won his second run over Stuefer by .041 of a second. And I was now the pro champion.

Everyone assumed I would now let up and rest on my laurels. But I still hadn't won a slalom all season, and I wasn't going to stop trying now.

Unfortunately, Tyler Palmer had some other ideas about it. He desperately wanted to win to show his boss that he was worth his contract money. For the Lange team racer to win the Lange Cup would have been especially sweet both to Tyler and to the Lange people. And now that I had the title, it seemed that no one was rooting for me anymore. The crowd was all his way, and Tyler pleased them with an excellent first run to beat me by .042 of a second.

"Palmer, you're fantastic," people were screaming.

Now, I don't mind saying that if there was anyone on the tour I *didn't* want to lose to in a head-to-head race, it was Tyler Palmer. He had made some very stupid remarks about me after my first race, and he and his brother Terry were always talking about "that fuckin' Frenchman." Their whole style of life was the opposite of mine. Frankly, Tyler's antics rubbed me the wrong way. I didn't think having this kind of person win would be good for the tour or good for the sport.

So in our second run, tired as I was, I went out for blood.

Gaylord Guenin, the managing editor of *Ski Racing,* and a pretty astute observer of the pro circuit, had written that when Tyler was skiing well, there wasn't anybody faster. This was one of those days when Tyler was skiing well. But there *was* somebody faster. I took the second run by .233 of a second—enough to put me into the finals.

In the other semifinal, Otto Tschudi, who was now assured of

fifth over Alain Penz, was facing Lasse Hamre. Hamre was last
year's Lange Cup winner, and it must have been the memory
of that victory that inspired him, because he was skiing better
than he had all year. Tschudi ran out of gas and disqualified.
"I took eleven vitamin pills this morning," he commented, "and
I think I just burned them all out at once. I had nothing left."

Tschudi wasn't the only one to complain about the course.
Stuefer admitted he was completely finished after his last run.
Penz also said, "I was just too tired." And the Canadian Bob
Swan commented, "That course was ten seconds too long."

But I was supposed to be the one who was out of shape, the
one who didn't have the strength or the stamina. At 8,000 feet,
running over 400 gates—which is what it took to win—was
like running twice that many at an area like Mt. Snow, let's
say, which had its course set at barely over 1,000 feet above
sea level. And that many gates is about four times what an
amateur runs, too. I was really tired. I can't deny that.

But Hamre was even more tired. And he ran into some bad
luck, too. He lost the baskets off both his poles at the top of
the course, and after the first run, I was ahead by more than
a second. I figured all I would have to do would be to stand
up through the finish line on the next run, and I would have
my first slalom victory.

Hamre knew it, and he knew he had to go all out to overtake
me. On the final jump, he was just pushing too hard and blew
off the course to disqualify. "There were just too many gates,"
he gasped at the finish line.

Michel, Danièle, my father—they were all beside themselves
with joy. Michel had been working all season long to get a pair
of slalom skis that would perform consistently well for me, to
fix my boots so I would have no pain and still have control—
and here was the payoff. I was very happy, too, of course. It
should have been the kind of sensation I had experienced at
Mt. Snow—and before that at the Hahnenkamm and at Portillo. But it wasn't.

Maybe I was too tired. Or maybe it was because I immediately had to go back up for a runoff with Stuefer for the Lange
Cup, worth an additional $2,500. If the same man doesn't win

the slalom and giant slalom, then the two winners must face each other to decide who gets the cup.

It was sort of anticlimactic for me. I was exhausted, while Stuefer, who had been eliminated in the quarterfinals, had had two rounds to rest up. Nevertheless, in our head-to-head meetings over the season, I had not yet beaten Stuefer, and I figured it would be the end of a perfect day if I could now add the Lange Cup runoff to my other victories.

It was an exciting race. For forty-five gates, we were almost neck and neck. Michel says I was actually slightly ahead. But, six gates from the end, I caught a tip and fell. Frankly, if I hadn't fallen, I don't know if I could have won. I had passed my limit.

But it didn't really matter that much. That night, at the Benson & Hedges banquet, I was the one who walked away with the $40,000 top prize. Added to my tour winnings of $28,625, that wasn't a bad pot. Stuefer, in second place, had $20,000 added to his tour winnings of $25,575. Spider's third place total came to $36,550, which wasn't too bad, either. All of us, of course, had additional sponsors' contracts, though nobody else on the tour had anything like the promotional contracts I had—which meant not only that nobody else was earning what I was, but that no other competitor had to spend the kind of time I spent making commercials, public appearances, and the like.

That evening at the Benson & Hedges banquet, Bob Beattie got me to drink more than I am accustomed to, and I guess seeing me a bit tipsy made some of the other racers accept me more as one of their own. Or maybe, now that it was over, they could see more clearly how much my presence had added to the tour. The attitude earlier had seemed to be, "We built it up and now you walk in and take all the glory." Some reflection made it clear that the circuit could attract big names only when it was profitable for the big names to join.

Now that Bleiner is joining, it is only a matter of time before Thoeni, Russel, Augert, Zwilling, and the other top amateurs will be coming on board. And then it will be really interesting.

And there will also be young racers, who haven't made it in

the amateurs, coming into the pro circuit and suddenly blossoming, just as Otto Tschudi, Dan Mooney, and Perry Thompson did this past year. I think, though, that as the pro league matures, it will be mostly the established names that join the circuit. They'll be able to negotiate better deals than the unknowns, and therefore, there will be more of an incentive to make a name first in the amateurs.

I'm in favor of keeping the age limit in the pros at twenty-one. The professional circuit should not be in competition with the amateur, but a logical progression up from it.

Will this kind of skiing take hold in Europe? I think there is no question it will. The Europeans are greater ski fans—spectator ski fans, that is—than the Americans. Once they realize that this format gives them the opportunity to see their favorites not just for one fleeting moment, but over and over again during a day, they will go wild for this kind of racing.

Some critics say the absence of downhill would kill interest in Europe. I don't think that's true because there is plenty of spectator excitement in this sport the way it is—with its built-in jumps, the head-to-head parallel courses, the buildup to the last round (instead of the race being over once the first seed has run). But in any event, I don't think downhill is precluded from a pro tour. It would not be downhill as we know it in the amateurs, but it could be quite exciting. It would have to be shorter than the famous downhills because I think the basic format that Beattie has worked out is sound: It must be short enough to be seen easily on TV.

Perhaps a parallel downhill could start out with a corridor for the first 150 yards, and maybe one guy could pull away or wait behind the other guy to take advantage of the air stream. The hill would have to be steeper than many of those in use for slalom and giant slalom, but it wouldn't have to go more than 1,000 vertical feet or so. It could still involve wax problems, choice of line—everything the amateur downhills have except the big vertical.

A downhill that took about a minute to run would be ideal. You could run that nine times in a day and still not be exhausted. I think it could work well, and I wouldn't be at all surprised to see something like this in the next couple of seasons.

The European ski establishment, of course, is dead set against professional racing. The powers that be in the official federations would like to keep it a strictly American phenomenon. That may be one reason why there are not going to be any more World Cup races in the United States. As it was, the World Cup was never very big in the United States. The Europeans are perfectly happy to keep amateur skiing a European affair and let Beattie have his nice little tour.

The trouble is, once the equipment manufacturers begin to realize how much more they can get out of supporting professional racing, the amateurs will have less importance for them. Once the equipment manufacturers start abandoning amateur racing, open racing is inevitable. And if we get open racing, I think it could spell the end of ISRA, at least as a purely American circuit.

Bob Beattie has other problems besides potential competition from open racing in Europe. Since open racing may never materialize, probably his biggest worry right now is that he is so dependent on Benson & Hedges. If somebody in Benson & Hedges should suddenly decide ski racing—or this particular kind of ski racing—isn't the best way for that company to spend its advertising monies, Beattie would have to dig up another sponsor ready to put that much prize money into the kitty—or give up any idea of attracting top amateur ski stars.

I don't say it would be hard to find another sponsor. I think interest in professional ski racing is growing, and Benson & Hedges as well as other sponsors will get their promotional money's worth. But Beattie's outfit may be trying to do too many things to guarantee that the money will always be there.

Among the things that Beattie does is represent some of the skiers in the same way that Mark McCormack represents me. Nothing wrong with that—except that ISRA, which is supposed to represent all the racers, is also Beattie's property. Spider Sabich is Beattie's client, so one would see ISRA releases in the course of the season paying more than an appropriate amount of attention to the exploits of Sabich. That's a minor thing, of course. But there is a legitimate question to be raised here. Is it not a conflict of interest to have the group that represents all the competitors also represent individuals among them?

I can't say I suffered from Beattie's representing a rival of mine. Oh, there were times when he was announcing a race when he would make comments like, "Notice that Jean-Claude is much faster than anyone else down here on the flats," as though I had not also been much faster up on the steep section. But in the heat of a match, no announcer can be really analytical, and Bob does a pretty fair job.

There were reports, in fact, that Beattie had made a special deal with me, and that contrary to ISRA rules, I was getting paid appearance money. Apart from my contracts with manufacturers, my prize money was the only money I made from racing on the ISRA tour. I can state that categorically. I think the crowds that came out to watch me and the press attention the circuit got because of me indicate that appearance money would not have been unreasonable. But the ISRA rules did not permit it.

Suppose that a whole bunch of top amateurs should decide to join the tour, how would I do against them? The only way I can answer that convincingly is on the race course. But I'm not in any doubt about the outcome.

Last season, Michel kept a chart showing how each of the racers finished in every event. Some people seeing that chart thought, "This guy just tries to give himself something to do. He's playing games trying to make ski competition look scientific."

Well, Michel doesn't just play games with his charts. He studies every racer's performance to see whether there are patterns he can discern related to the weather, the snow conditions, whether it's early or late in the season, the type of course, and so forth. Neither Michel nor I believe much in luck. If you get a lucky break and you're not prepared to take advantage of it, it won't be lucky for you.

From his charts, Michel could see what kind of training I had to do for my second season. He could see whether I needed to take chances and go all out facing this skier or could relax and ski cautiously facing that one. We leave nothing to chance. Instead of starting off the season looking desperately for the right equipment, now we know what will do the job.

No other competitors that I know—amateur or professional— have this kind of systematic approach to getting the maximum out of themselves and their equipment. So it is more than simply my own ego that gives me this confidence.

Of course, nobody can go on forever. I am thirty years old now, and perhaps the reflexes of a twenty-four-year-old will prove superior to mine. But he'll need more than fast reflexes. He'll have to have the same kind of determination, the same kind of concentration, the same kind of perfectionism, the same kind of expertise on equipment, the same kind of refusal to accept defeat.

Then, maybe a younger man will beat me.

So far, I don't see anyone like that on the slopes.